Phenomenal Female Entrepreneurs

The Women's Hall of Fame Series

Phenomenal Female Entrepreneurs

JILL BRYANT

Second Story Press

Library and Archives Canada Cataloguing in Publication

Bryant, Jill, author
Phenomenal female entrepreneurs / Jill Bryant.

(Women's hall of fame series)
Issued in print and electronic formats.
ISBN 978-1-927583-12-8 (pbk.) ISBN 978-1-927583-13-5 (epub)

1. Businesswomen—Biography—Juvenile literature. 2. Women
executives—Biography—Juvenile literature. 3.Entrepreneurship—
Juvenile literature. I. Title. II. Series: Women's hall of fame series

HD6054.3.B79 2013   j338.092'52
C2013-903875-2
C2013-903876-0

Editor: Kathryn White
Designer: Melissa Kaita
Cover photos and icons © iStockphoto

Printed and bound in Canada

*Second Story Press gratefully acknowledges the support of the
Ontario Arts Council and the Canada Council for the Arts for our
publishing program. We acknowledge the financial support of the
Government of Canada through the Canada Book Fund.*

Published by
Second Story Press
20 Maud Street, Suite 401
Toronto, ON
M5V 2M5
www.secondstorypress.ca

For Zoë, Mari, and Rhea – believe in your crazy ideas

Contents

Introduction

Entrepreneurs are vital to society. They create companies, foster relationships, develop skills, and lead teams. The companies and projects they start enrich people's lives and provide much-needed jobs. Their profits help improve the wealth, or economy, of a region. Companies built by entrepreneurs produce all kinds of products and services that people need – or think they need. Some entrepreneurs also strive to make the world a better place. They give back to the community in deeply meaningful ways.

As leaders in business, entrepreneurs can influence people and bring about positive change. For example, some of the entrepreneurs profiled in this book have spoken out for civil rights. Others have defied stereotypes, sparked social change, and improved people's health and sense of well-being – and the list goes on. To be sure, many entrepreneurs are motivated to do much more than make money.

Born in the late 1800s, self-made millionaire Madam C.J. Walker and retail president Dorothy Shaver were trailblazers in their contributions to women in business. Dame Anita Roddick, founder of The Body Shop, and high-finance expert Naina Lal Kidwai were also ahead of their time, showing they could build profitable businesses based on honesty, trust, fairness, responsibility, and respect. The next wave of women entrepreneurs, now in their 30s and 40s, has gained strength in numbers (hurray!) – numbers that are climbing higher and faster than ever before. Sheryl Sandberg, Sue Chen, Susan Mashibe, Nicole Robertson, Kelsey Ramsden, and Jodi Glover are excellent examples, and there are many others. In spite of the fact that momentum is finally growing, and more women are attaining top-tier roles, there is still a gap. The fact is, women do make excellent entrepreneurs and business leaders. It's time to fix the imbalance. Be bold, be confident, work hard, and make your special vision come to life.

Most entrepreneurs are ideas people. They excel at brainstorming and are keen to pursue their sometimes wild, often crazy, ideas. They aren't afraid to try something new and take a risk. Entrepreneurs learn from their mistakes and

Head-Scratcher Stats

In Canada, the number of self-employed women is on the rise, and remarkably, four out of five new businesses are led by women. But while women have owned nearly half of all the small- and mid-sized businesses for the past five years, only 17 percent hold high-level corporate positions. In the United States, women own less that 30 percent of all businesses and make up just 15 percent of the top-tier jobs. On the other hand, women are very well-educated, earning about 60 percent of the bachelor's and master's degrees. In the world at large, this same, strange pattern of inequality persists. What's going on? The trend is puzzling, for sure.

keep moving forward. They are passionate about their careers and work hard to see their dreams take flight. They are well-organized and they are good planners, but they aren't afraid of scrapping yesterday's plan and pursuing a

Social Entrepreneur

This is a highly motivated business owner who wants to improve an aspect of society or the environment. These individuals are committed to making the world a better place through their business. Save the planet!

new vision, if necessary. They are adept at sidestepping to move with changes in the marketplace. In addition, entrepreneurs tend to view problems as positives, tackling them expertly and creatively. They rarely let problems drag them down. Instead, they take pleasure in finding effective solutions that make their businesses stand apart from the competition – and grow.

The ten women you'll read about in this book possess remarkable traits that have helped them succeed and gain recognition for their achievements in business. These female entrepreneurs also share some key experiences:

At least two entrepreneurs – Kelsey Ramsden and Jodi Glover – were enterprising as kids.

As high school students, Dorothy Shaver, Naina Lal Kidwai, Nicole Robertson, Kelsey Ramsden, and Jodi Glover loved team sports.

In their graduating classes, Naina Lal Kidwai, Sue Chen, and Sheryl Sandberg were top students and involved in student politics.

Three of the women – Sheryl Sandberg, Sue Chen, and Kelsey Ramsden – swear there's no such thing as work-life balance. Instead, it's a matter of focusing on the tasks that are most urgent at any given moment.

Seven out of the ten female entrepreneurs are mothers. Kelsey Ramsden and Jodi Glover – both in their 30s – took only

8 Winning Characteristics of Successful Entrepreneurs

- Independent: I like my own ideas

- Ambitious: I will make my dream come true

- Determined: I think I can, I know I can

- Hard-Working: I like to work hard

- Passionate: I love what I do!

- Self-Confident: I can do it!

- Strong Leader: I can build a motivated team

- Adaptable: I can try again

two or three days off work when their babies were born.

Naina Lal Kidwai, Sheryl Sandberg, and Kelsey Ramsden faced situations on the job in which they were the only women and had to sort out fundamental basics, like where the women's washroom was. Sometimes their male colleagues didn't know.

Many people thought Susan Mashibe, Sue Chen, and Jodi Glover would close up shop after a short time in business. Instead, they went on to succeed.

Learn from these phenomenal entrepreneurs and then develop your own vision. Whatever you strive for, stay true to your passion. And, last but not least: have fun with whatever you choose to pursue.

Madam C.J. Walker

1867 - 1919

A hush falls over the crowd. The fundraising campaign offi-cially begins today – Monday, October 23, 1910. Yesterday, two white businessmen made generous gifts. Now, the African American community wants to prove they can help, too. The funds will be used to build a new YMCA, where young African American men can sleep comfortably and enjoy hot meals. But in this time of racial inequality, most black workers earn mea-ger incomes. Still, the energetic crowd of African Americans gathered today feels duty-bound to play their part. They will give what they can.

Standing tall, her shoulders squared, Madam C.J. Walker, businesswoman and owner of the successful Madam C.J.

Walker Manufacturing Company, acknowledges the crowd with a respectful nod. "I pledge $1,000," she says confidently. Excited cries erupt from the assembly. Three hundred people shout, clap, shriek, and stomp their feet. The immaculately groomed, heavy-set woman smiles broadly and continues, "If the association can save our boys, our girls will be saved, and that's what I am interested in." She goes on to explain her own desire to create an association for African American girls.

Sitting back down, she smooths the long folds in her floor-length skirt, crossing her lace-up boots at the ankle. Currently earning $1,000 a month, Madam Walker will be stretching her financial resources thin. But she is determined to honor her word. Her proud smile remains as she listens to her fellow African Americans make a series of additional pledges. Hope and joy prevail.

Madam Walker was a successful entrepreneur and woman of affluence, but it wasn't always that way. She was born on a cotton plantation in Delta, Louisiana, on December 23, 1867. In those days she was called Sarah Breedlove. The Breedlove family was extremely poor, and Sarah's home was nothing more than a one-room, tumble-down shack.

Situated northwest of New Orleans and west of Jackson, Mississippi, Sarah's birthplace was near the banks of the Mississippi River. Riverboats, heaped high with cotton, passed up and down the congested river, transporting goods from the Deep South to the northern reaches of the country. Back then, when people needed water for cooking or washing, they hand pumped a bucketful from a well, or scooped it from the river. Poor families had to do this several times each day.

Sarah's parents worked as sharecroppers. They were hard-working farmers who toiled from morning to night, working the land that belonged to a white landowner. After cultivating cotton, they were obliged to give the landowner a large portion of their crops or earnings. This arrangement would leave Owen and Minerva Breedlove with very little money of their own to feed and clothe their six children. Prior to becoming sharecroppers, the Breedloves were slaves. In fact, baby Sarah was the only child in the Breedlove family who was born into freedom. Even so, she entered a world where most African Americans in the South were treated terribly – without the dignity and respect all humans deserve. It was no longer permitted to own slaves, but the new practices were a far cry from true freedom or emancipation. Her parents and siblings continued working in the cotton fields, just as they had when they were slaves. The only difference was that now they earned a meager wage. Sarah worked in the fields alongside her sister, from morning 'til night. Carrying water, planting seeds, and feeding chickens were other tasks Sarah was expected to do. Each year, the landowner gave the sharecropper children enough fabric to make a single dress. Sarah had only the bare necessities – nothing extra.

Sarah's parents both died of serious diseases when she was seven. After that she was raised by her sister, Louvenia, and her loathsome brother-in-law, Jesse Powell. They lived across the river from the cotton plantation in the city of Vicksburg. To earn money, Sarah washed clothes for white families. At the young age of 14, Sarah married laborer Moses McWilliams. She was relieved to get away from her cruel brother-in-law and to have a home of her own. Her daughter Lelia was born when Sarah was 17. The young mother pledged to give her baby daughter a better life. Then, at last, an abundant cotton harvest allowed farm workers to treat themselves to a few extras. Sarah had hope for the future. But Moses died unexpectedly – perhaps in an accident, or by the hand of a murderer. The young mother couldn't waste time feeling sorry for herself. She had to earn a living to support herself and her toddler-age daughter.

Hair loss was another hardship that plagued Sarah in her

20s. How upsetting it was to see bald patches appearing on her head! She was not alone. Most poor women lived without the luxury of running water. As a result, they only washed their hair about once a month. Infrequent washing and poor nutrition led to itchy, irritated scalps – and eventually, scalp diseases. Dull, brittle, and limp hair was the norm among most African American women. Indeed, some scholars say that hair, which is often an expression of beauty and pride, became an outward symbol of black women's low status in nineteenth-century society. It's fair to say that many black women were not very proud of their hair. Wealthy white women, in contrast, ate healthier foods and typically boasted more manageable, shiny tresses.

When Sarah heard that wages were higher in the big city of St. Louis, she and her three-year-old daughter traveled north by riverboat, arriving at this busy port city on the eastern edge of the state of Missouri. Family ties drew her there as well. Her three older brothers were employed in St. Louis as barbers. While seeking work as a washerwoman, Sarah made sure her well-worn clothes were clean and neatly pressed. After all, wouldn't this help advertise her laundry services?

Sarah worked as a laundress, putting in grueling 14-hour days for many years. Her work involved soaking clothes in tubs of warm water, scrubbing each garment vigorously on a washboard, rubbing the clothing with lye-based soap, and then boiling, rinsing, and hanging the clothes to dry. Heaving vats of water and carrying mounds of laundry was physically exhausting. The soap made her hands sting. In spite of these hardships, Sarah did her job well. She was determined to give her daughter a better life, so she lived frugally on her $1.50-a-week earnings and saved for Lelia's education. Just before Lelia finished high school, Sarah divorced John Davis, her second husband of nine years. This failed marriage did not deplete her finances, however. Independent-minded Sarah had learned not to depend on others for matters concerning money. Instead, she boldly took it upon herself to earn enough money to feed and clothe her growing child.

Throughout Sarah's employment as a washerwoman, she was watchful of what was going on around her. Life was not easy for African Americans. In spite of what she saw, Sarah kept a positive outlook. After all, because of her

What's In a Name?

"Madam," like "Mrs.," was a title of respect for women, taken from the French. In the field of cosmetics and fashion, the French are highly respected and accomplished. The title had an exotic, foreign air to it, which appealed to Sarah. Once she settled on this name for herself and the brand of her products, she stuck with it. (Brand identity is an important marketing strategy that savvy entrepreneurs embrace today, perhaps even more so than they did in the past.) Her products – and her name – soon became widely recognized.

hard work and frugal ways, her daughter would receive a fine education. As Lelia neared adulthood, Sarah kept her eyes open for new opportunities. She attended night school and learned to read and write. Washing clothes was not her true calling – of that she was certain. This budding entrepreneur was due for a change.

Trying out different shampoos and ointments had become a pastime for Sarah. She experimented with a homemade product named "Poro," created by Annie Pope Turnbo (later called Annie Malone). Poro products contained sulfur – an ingredient, with antibacterial and healing properties – that nourishes dry skin and controls dandruff. The products made her scalp healthier and her hair more manageable. Sarah was sold! She accepted a job as a cook at a boarding house in Denver, Colorado. She also signed on as a sales representative for Annie in 1905, at age 38. Her life was in transition, and she was very pleased about this. She happily touted Annie's hair products to other African American women and saved up some more money.

In 1906, she married her third husband, a newspaper advertising salesman named Charles Joseph Walker. Determined to create her own hair-care recipe, Sarah altered the ingredients in Annie's products and launched her own Wonderful Hair Grower. Sarah and her salesman husband, C.J. Walker, traveled extensively, selling this 35-cent product door-to-door and pitching to crowds of women. Her other goods included Vegetable Shampoo and Vanishing Cream. Black women were excited about trying her products and delighted with the results. Sarah, now known as Madam C.J. Walker – a name she would keep – had found a product that women wanted, and *she* was supplying it. Her great business idea was taking flight.

Madam C.J. Walker's Wonderful Hair Grower catered to African American women and promoted pride in healthy, well-groomed hair. By 1925, the date of this tin, the price had risen to 50 cents.

Madam Walker called herself a "hair culturist." She was not obsessed, like many others, with altering hair to be more like the hair of Caucasians. Instead, she promoted thick, healthy hair through good grooming and the use of her high-quality products. She was devoted to her female clientele, who were mainly African Americans. The secret to her success was really hard work.

Although her husband was against the idea, Madam Walker chose Pittsburgh, a transportation hub, as the site of the new company headquarters in 1908. Sarah hired her 23-year-old daughter to take the helm there. In 1910, Madam Walker moved on to Indianapolis, Indiana – the "Railroad City," with 200 passenger trains each day – where she founded the Madam C.J. Walker Manufacturing Company. Her company provided steady work for 3,000 African Americans. She also set up a school of cosmetics called Lelia College, where her daughter, a proud graduate of Knoxville College, trained students in good grooming, hygiene, beauty, and hair care. Upon graduation, the women became "hair culturists" and enjoyed respectable careers as Walker agents. Sarah took great interest in her thousands of, mostly female, employees. She offered conventions and clubs to provide further opportunities for learning, networking, and making friends. Walker agents could be recognized by their respectable, long black skirts and crisp white blouses. Perhaps her greatest ambition, though, was to motivate her workforce to action. Supporting civil rights and opposing racist policies were Madam's true passion.

Churches and community halls made ideal places for finding talented and outgoing women. Women who were looking for new job opportunities were happy to join Madam Walker's company as recruiting agents. In this unjust era, the job prospects for African American women were limited to washerwoman, maid, cook, sharecropper, or factory worker. None of these options paid much more than a dollar a day. Female

Walker agents, on the other hand, often earned more in one day than white men earned in a full week! They had choices, too. They could earn money by selling products door-to-door or by offering beauty treatments.

Madam Walker's mail-order business was hugely successful, and she was keen to keep expanding. Business was thriving. In the meantime, her imagination was brimming over with ways she could spend – or, rather, invest – her money. Cars? A mansion? Fine clothing? Some of these possessions appealed to her, sure, but only insofar as they showed her fellow African American citizens that they, too, could aspire to greatness. More importantly, she wanted to give back to

Damsels of Direct Marketing

- Annie Pope Turnbo Malone (1869 – 1957) launched Poro Products, a cosmetics firm, and hired sales reps to sell her products door-to-door just four years before Madam C.J. Walker launched her own brand

- Brownie Wise (1913 – 1992), Tupperware executive, developed and promoted the "home party" as a marketing means for hired "party hostesses" to sell plastic food-storage containers

- Mary Kay Ash (1918 – 2001) invested $5,000 in the formulas for skin-care products in 1963, hired salespeople, and used direct marketing to build a cosmetics empire known as Mary Kay Inc.

- Doris K. Christopher (1945 –) founded her business in the 1980s to demonstrate and market The Pampered Chef kitchen tools in people's kitchens

- Janet Rickstrew (1962 –) and Mary Tatum (1965 –) of Tomboy Tools have sales agents attend home parties to teach women to do home repairs and show off the company's snazzy tools.

the black community by building schools, giving scholarships, financing education for children, and donating money to civil-rights charities. She also had the notion that, as a rich business owner, she could use her elevated position in society to bring about

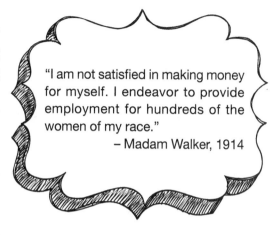

"I am not satisfied in making money for myself. I endeavor to provide employment for hundreds of the women of my race."
– Madam Walker, 1914

change. She wanted to make life safer for her people, and to help them earn respect and win fair wages.

Again, her husband tried to hold her back. He thought she should be satisfied with more modest earnings and leave it at that. Madam Walker once explained, "When I started in

Madam C.J. Walker took great pleasure in proudly driving her own car. In this picture, taken around 1916, her niece and two employees are enjoying a ride.

business...with my husband, I had business disagreements with him.... I was convinced that my hair preparations would fill a long-felt want, and when we found it impossible to agree, due to his narrowness of vision, I embarked in business for myself." Thus, it's not surprising that, in 1912, her third marriage also ended in divorce.

Now that she was such an established and respected figure in the business world, Madam Walker was invited to attend numerous meetings for African American groups and associations. She herself was frequently asked to speak at public venues, often in black churches. Madam Walker inspired others with her words. She made a point of attending a particular meeting of the National Negro Business League (NNBL) in 1912. Held in Chicago, this was a formal gathering of the most successful and powerful African American entrepreneurs in the United States. There was one catch, however. The speakers – and most members – were male. Even though Madam Walker was now highly respected among many business leaders, in this particular venue she was utterly and completely ignored by the group's founder. The crafty and influential educator Booker T. Washington refused to let Madam Walker address the crowd. Proud of her accomplishments and determined to make her voice heard, Madam Walker rose from her chair and proclaimed confidently to the crowd, "I am a woman who came from the cotton fields of the South. From there I was promoted to the washtub. From there I was promoted to the cook kitchen. And from there, I promoted myself into

Bessie Coleman (1892 – 1926) turned to barber shops when she ran out of money at college in 1915. For a time she was known as "the best and fastest manicurist in Chicago," before pursuing her true dream of becoming an aerial daredevil pilot. She opted to earn her pilot's license in France, where racism was less widespread.

the business of manu- facturing hair goods and preparations. I have built my own fac- tory on my own ground." A quiet hush followed this beautifully crafted, intelligent, and highly effective speech. The next year, without hesitation, Booker T. Washington invited her to partici- pate in the meeting as a guest speaker. Madam had made it clear: she was not a woman to be ignored!

In 1913, Madam Walker bought property

Dress for Success

Women seeking new jobs don't always have a business outfit hanging in their closet, or enough cash to go shopping for dress pants, a blouse, and a blazer. This not-for-profit organization called Dress for Success, founded in New York City in 1997, provides women who have a scheduled job interview with a coordinated and professional outfit – at no cost. Established pro- fessional businesswomen donate clothing to this charity. Wearing proper business attire to an interview can give women with financial challenges the opportunity they need to apply their skills, advance their careers, and rise out of poverty.

in New York City – in Harlem, an area populated by African Americans. Lelia renovated the buildings into a Walker beauty parlor and a beauty school and ran these two businesses. In the meantime, Madam Walker's sister, Louvenia, worked in the Indianapolis factory, while two nieces had a Walker agency in Los Angeles. It was important to Madam Walker to assist and encourage the women in her family, and to lend a hand to her fellow African Americans.

Remarkably, by 1915, just five years after formally reg- istering her manufacturing company, and nine years after creating her own brand of hair-care products, Madam Walker had become the richest African American women in the United States.

In 1916, sales soared even higher. By this time, Madam C.J. Walker employed 20,000 agents. Due to her extensive sales trips, her company now spanned the United States and extended into Canada and countries throughout the Caribbean and South America. Average earnings were $23 a week for Walker agents, which was nearly $5 a week more than a decent factory job paid – in the North. In the South, the situation for factory workers was even more dire, with black workers earning a mere $4 a week. Sure, Madam Walker could have paid her Walker agents less, but this would have gone against her honest character. Instead, she paid handsomely, giving her sales reps financial security. She even organized a union for the workers. These privileges allowed Walker employees to gain self-confidence and take great pride in their work. Madam C.J. Walker inspired other African American women to be entrepreneurs. She also encouraged people to join together for worthy causes. In fact, she offered cash incentives to her own workers for the highest number of hours of community service.

Madam Walker was now earning $1,000 a week, yet she wasted no time in basking in the luxuries of life. Instead, she focused on putting an end to lynching, a terrible hate crime in which a mob kills someone. (Thousands of African Americans were murdered in this manner.) Madam Walker left people flabbergasted when she donated a staggering $5,000 to this movement. It was by far the biggest donation.

Madam C.J. Walker, the ground-breaking entrepreneur, self-made millionaire, generous philanthropist, and civil rights activist, died on May 25th, 1919. She was 51. True to her giving nature, she left most of her money to charities. Certainly Madam Walker, who brought gainful employment to black women across the United States and beyond, helped propel the civil rights movement. By building a business based on quality and honesty, and by reinvesting in the people who supported her business, Madam C.J. Walker made positive changes that revolutionized what it meant to be free and equal in American society.

Dorothy Shaver

1893 - 1959

B ehind the glass of deep-set department store windows, small figures – wearing old-fashioned wool coats, tweed caps, and fluffy muffs – skate on a silvery pond. In another window, a speaker projects the song "Parade of the Wooden Soldiers" out onto the street while a carousel, filled with ginger-bread boys and girls, dolls, soldiers, and teddy bears, turns slowly. Meanwhile, outside, standing on the sidewalk, excited children press their noses against the glass. They watch the imaginative storefront scenes, mesmerized.

Long before the invention of interactive games and home entertainment systems, beautifully decorated Christmas windows amused crowds of people in big cities such as New York.

Dorothy Shaver, who spent 35 years working on Fifth Avenue at Lord & Taylor, was a pioneer in window dressing. She collaborated with designers and window dressers to create inviting displays that told a story, conjured a mood, or evoked a happy memory. For her, decorated windows were much more than places to display high stacks of products. Rather, they were a way of capturing attention and presenting an attractive lifestyle. Ultimately, of course, window displays enticed curious customers into the store. Throughout her long and successful career, Dorothy believed that department stores should be beautiful, inside and out. The marble floors, vaulted ceilings, breathtaking chandeliers, and mannequins dressed in the latest fashions all worked together to create an enjoyable shopping experience.

Dorothy's modern ideas succeeded in bringing thousands of visitors into Lord & Taylor. Some came in just to browse, but others pulled out their pocketbooks and spent money – a trinket here, an outfit there. Sales increased, and Lord & Taylor prospered. Dorothy's efforts did not go unrecognized. Over the years, she was promoted again and again.

Dorothy Shaver was born in 1893 in Center Point, a small town in Arkansas. Her parents, James and Sally, were well-known in the community, and her family was fairly wealthy. When Dorothy was five, her family moved to Mena, a newly formed town, also in Arkansas. Her father opened a law practice and, years later, became a judge. James was a respected leader in Mena and involved in local politics.

As a child, Dorothy was outgoing and had many friends. She was fond of lots of different activities, including sports. For example, Dorothy often played baseball with boys in her neighborhood. She also sang in a church choir.

In 1910, at age 17, Dorothy graduated from Mena High School. She was chosen from among all her classmates to deliver a speech to the graduating class. A couple of years later, Dorothy earned a teaching certificate from the University of Arkansas in Fayetteville. Then, she returned to Mena and taught grade seven students at the local elementary school.

Dorothy was a competent teacher, but her active social life raised the ire of members of the school board. They considered it scandalous that Dorothy dared to go out without a chaperone. At that time, the rules of proper conduct decreed that unmarried women were not to venture into public spaces without an escort.

When Dorothy was 21, some members of the school board heard that she had attended a dance without a chaperone. This was too much for the small-town officials to endure. Her improper behavior left the school board with no other options. Dorothy's teaching contract was not renewed. In short, she was dismissed.

Clearly, Mena was not the place for Dorothy to stay. In 1916, she and her younger sister, Elsie, moved to Chicago. Years earlier, in 1893, Chicago had been the site of the hugely influential World's Fair. The effect of the World's Fair upon the city was profound. Art, culture, architecture, food – and new products of all kinds – were all showcased for the attending visitors. Twenty-three years later, the effect of the World's Fair lingered. Chicago was a proud city, and its people seemed to be more cultured and worldly. Many young people who wanted adventure were attracted to this famous city. Certainly, Dorothy and her sister would enjoy greater freedom in Chicago, the second-largest city in the United States.

Dorothy, who was 23 years old, didn't know what she wanted to do with her life, but a fresh start in a big city seemed fitting. The two sisters found an apartment and enrolled at the University of Chicago. Elsie focused on painting while Dorothy studied English literature. Money wasn't a concern; they had family resources to support themselves.

After close to a year in Chicago, the sisters yearned for more excitement and change. They traveled to New York City, found a place to live, and settled in. New York was a huge center for manufacturing, commerce, art, and culture. Life was definitely exciting, and change was everywhere.

Eventually, Dorothy started thinking about ways to earn a living. She considered Elsie's artistic skills and her own excellent people skills. Together, they could make a good team. Dorothy asked Elsie to design and sew a collection of rag dolls. Dorothy figured that if her sister could make them, she could sell them. Elsie created designs for five dolls, which she called the "Five Little Shavers." They had cloth bodies, yarn hair, and painted faces. Dorothy was impressed with the results and encouraged her sister to make more. Then, Dorothy presented the dolls to Samuel Reyburn, president of Lord & Taylor – an upscale department store on Fifth Avenue. Samuel, who was

Rag Dolls to Riches - Doll-Making Entrepreneurs

- Elders Susie Angootealak, Annie Nestor, and Natuk Pariyuk, Nunavut, Canada – Designing and sewing traditional Inuit dolls provides the three partners at Natuq's Sewing with a rewarding livelihood

- Kathleen Gibbs, Joy2theWorld.org, Ghana, West Africa – Selling handmade rag dolls helps secure loans for aspiring businesswomen in Ghana

- Stacey McBride-Irby, One World Doll Project, Houston/Los Angeles, U.S.A. – Designing culturally diverse dolls helps promote positive images that empower girls

- Nadia Hashimi, Afghan Dolls Project, Afghanistan – Creating female entrepreneurs is the aim of this business launched in 2003

a friend of the Shaver family, agreed to sell the "Five Little Shavers" at Lord & Taylor, provided Dorothy took charge of marketing the rag dolls. Dorothy was thrilled! This was just the break she and Elsie needed to help their business grow.

Dorothy had great ideas for promoting the delightful dolls – right in the store's front windows – and they sold well. The cuddly rag dolls quickly captured the attention of many admirers. In fact, they became a hugely popular fad. Dorothy spotted young women toting the dolls around on the streets of New York. They all wanted to be seen with the dolls. Dorothy and Elsie kept this business going for three years. Then, Elsie wanted to pursue painting, so they closed the doll business.

Samuel Reyburn noticed Dorothy's creativity and fearlessness in marketing the dolls. In 1921, he hired Dorothy (now 28) to head the "Comparison Bureau" at Lord & Taylor. This

The Five Little Shaver dolls, two painted here by Elsie Shaver, were a popular fad and a huge success, thanks to Dorothy's brilliant marketing.

department sounded important, but Dorothy's position was low in the store's chain of command. Her task was to write a business report. Samuel asked her to share information about clothing lines, prices, featured merchandise, and special promotions with Lord & Taylor managers. In this way, Dorothy would help the store become more knowledgeable about their competition. She began observing other department stores, collecting facts for her report.

Many others would take delight in getting paid to pretend-shop, while secretly jotting down prices, brand names, and store layouts, but Dorothy found this mission boring. In her report, she added her own bold recommendations and suggested renaming the division the "Bureau of Stylists." This name was more appealing and dynamic. Then, rather than dwelling on the marketing strategies of other stores, as she'd been instructed to do, Dorothy urged management to focus on "designing the right things to begin with." Certainly, by stretching above and beyond her new role, Dorothy hoped to impress the store's upper management. After all, she wasn't satisfied with staying in an entry-level position.

Dorothy's confidence and boldness paid off. In 1924, Samuel hired Dorothy, as a full-time employee, to set up a Bureau of Stylists, just as she had proposed. She sought out the best-quality goods for Lord & Taylor customers and provided store buyers with much more thorough product training. Next, she began to focus intently on the area that captivated her most: women's fashion.

Co-workers described Dorothy as "sizzling with ideas," which is easy to believe. By 1927, age 34, she'd advanced to director of the Lord & Taylor board, making her a central decision maker. In 1928, independent of Lord & Taylor, she co-founded the Fashion Group with 16 other women, all of whom were eager to promote American women in the fashion industry. In this same year, at Lord & Taylor, Dorothy planned a furniture and housewares exhibition that featured works by inventive French designers, including paintings by artists such as Pablo Picasso. The event was a tremendous success. It introduced New York to an elegant, sleek, and streamlined design concept known as Art Deco. This style

The Roaring Twenties

In the 1920s, times were good, and most folks had jobs, food, and money. In fact, the decade known as the "Roaring Twenties" was filled with celebration and luxury. In New York City, the best jazz and blues musicians in the country performed in popular nightclubs. The boom in business made real-estate prices soar. New buildings began stretching upward, rather than outward. The result was a new kind of skyline with tall skyscrapers, built for the richest companies.

had been featured already at the Paris World's Fair in 1925, but U.S. manufacturers and U.S. officials did not attend that particular fair, claiming they were not interested in modern designs. Meanwhile, the general public was keen to see this exciting, cutting-edge style. They attended the gala, which Dorothy planned, in droves.

Two months after Dorothy's successful exhibition at Lord & Taylor, Macy's department store staged its own French-style exhibition. Meanwhile, Dorothy was busy pondering her next move. One niggling question stood out: Why did the spotlight always have to be on *French* fashion?

Business-savvy Dorothy Shaver possessed remarkable foresight. During a time when French fashion reigned supreme, she successfully managed to shift the focus to American fashion. Dorothy saw great value in offering customers made-in-America style. After all, with the advent of the Great Depression in 1929, and the high rates of unemployment, the affluence of the twenties was gone. Times were tough and opportunities slim. At the same time, trained American designers were graduating each year, looking for work opportunities and a chance to earn a living in their fields. Dorothy viewed these graduates as a vast pool of talent, just waiting to be discovered. As it was, the only way these grads could make a name for themselves was to go to Paris. In her respected position, Dorothy believed she could change this. Quite simply, she would hire American designers. Then she would advertise their clothing to American customers. If her plan was successful, Lord & Taylor would produce higher profits, and more money would stay in the hands of U.S. employees

Designers Are Entrepreneurs, Too

During the Depression, Lord & Taylor sought out American designers to promote and feature in their store. This movement lasted well into the 1950s. Below are some of the first American designers who earned a living from their fashionable designs:

- Nettie Rosenstein (1890 – 1980) – Designer known for her little black dresses

- Lilly Daché (1898 – 1989) – Fashion designer and hat maker who created gowns and hats for Hollywood movie stars

- Muriel King (1900 – 1977) – Fashion designer known for reasonably priced, versatile outfits

- Clare Potter (1903 – 1999) – Inventor of American sportswear, for "town" or "country," made from easy-care synthetics and jersey-knit fabrics

- Elizabeth Hawes (1903 – 1971) – Designer of comfortable "ready to wear" (mass-produced) clothes

- Claire McCardell (1905 – 1958) – Designer who was known as the inventor of the "American Look"; created easy-wear dresses, the first mix-and-match separates, and featured lots of gingham

and entrepreneurs. Dorothy liked the sound of that.

Trailblazing Dorothy understood fashion and knew her customers well. She was convinced that American cus-tomers wanted good quality and dura-

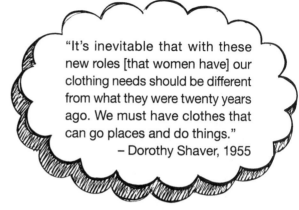

"It's inevitable that with these new roles [that women have] our clothing needs should be different from what they were twenty years ago. We must have clothes that can go places and do things."
– Dorothy Shaver, 1955

ble clothes that were reasonably priced. By hiring American fashion designers and promoting their clothing, Lord & Taylor could carve out an identity for itself as the department store that offered true American style. Dorothy was confident her idea was a winner, and she pursued its development, begin-ning in 1929. Her efforts were recognized and rewarded. In 1931, at age 38, Dorothy became a vice president in charge of style, publicity, and advertising.

Before getting into the nitty-gritty of commissioning dress design, Dorothy started her timely campaign by focusing on the fabric. She hired three talented American designers to cre-ate printed fabrics that would appeal to American women. The designers made dresses using their own fabrics for a spring promotion in 1932. Dorothy featured each designer's name beside her dress collection and hosted a lunch-time launch to promote the designers' work. On behalf of her team, Dorothy stated, "We believe that there must be clothes that are intrin-sically American and that only the American designer can create them."

Prior to the Second World War, fashionable women used to schedule up to three fittings at their dressmakers' for a garment as simple as a nightgown! With the new mass-pro-duced garments, however, fittings became a thing of the past,

Dorothy's fashion sense even went to war, helping American service women look smart and feel comfortable while serving their country.

reserved only for very special outfits, such as wedding gowns. With Dorothy's beautiful displays, reasonable prices, and clever marketing, she created a longing for a new look of irresistible, easy-wear, and easy-care clothing that women didn't even have on their wish lists. Why? Because American women had never seen clothing quite like this before.

Customers wanted these made-in-America designs that spoke to the wishes of "typical" American women. The clothes were more comfortable, casual,

Mmm... Smells Good!

Dorothy had a nose for good ideas. She once captured the attention of pedestrians with a giant atomizer that lightly sprayed perfume into the air. Smelling the wafting scents coming from above a department-store window, office workers on their lunch break could be lured into the Lord & Taylor store.

and better suited for working outside the home. Even though the outfits were mass-produced in factories, they boasted a personalized feel, simply because they were created specifically for American women. Being mass-produced, in a full range of sizes, also helped to keep the costs down, compared to the customized tailored outfits. "We sold 50 of one number and 150 of another in just a few days," explained Dorothy. "We were convinced that we had planned correctly and the American designers were at last coming into their own." Suddenly – almost overnight – gorgeous clothes were available to all women, at different price points. This was the beauty of mass production.

In 1937, at the height of the Depression, 44-year-old Dorothy Shaver advanced to first vice president at Lord & Taylor. She was earning an astronomical $75,000 a year – worth well over a million dollars in today's money. Remarkably, Dorothy's salary was comparable to salaries earned by men in executive positions at that time. Always breaking new ground, and wanting the company to continue to grow, Dorothy then proposed opening a branch store on Long Island.

Dorothy generously applauded the fashion media for their role in supporting American designers. *Vogue* magazine began publishing "Americana" issues every February, beginning in 1938. Likewise, fashion journalists and magazine editors further supported this trend. But Dorothy didn't leave it at that. As vice president at Lord & Taylor, she kept on pushing and promoting and looking out for American designers. It was important to her that designers were gainfully employed, respected, and revered. In 1938, Dorothy launched Lord & Taylor's Rose Awards to recognize Americans for their contributions to textile and clothing design. All of these diverse efforts, by many people, meant that American fashion flourished. The two Lord & Taylor stores enjoyed excellent sales during the difficult years of the Second World War.

In 1940, Lord & Taylor launched a Designer's Shop that featured styles by ten American designers. Dorothy oversaw the redesign of more comfortable and functional clothing for women serving overseas (often as nurses or clerical workers). At last, pants were an acceptable option in women's full-dress or daily-wear uniforms. During the war years, the government promoted "buying American," which further strengthened the whole notion of American clothing that was designed, manufactured, and sold in the United States. In fact, New York City became known as a new fashion capital in the world, on a par with Paris, Milan, and London. New York has maintained this honored title ever since.

In December 1945, when Walter Hoover resigned as president of Lord & Taylor, the board made an exciting announcement. In what was quoted as a "breathtaking first," the board chose the market-savvy, creative, and visionary Dorothy Shaver to take Walter's place. Thus, Dorothy, now

52, became the first female to head a Fifth Avenue department store. She had climbed the corporate ladder to success; she held this role for 14 years. What's more, she had earned this position through her own hard work, loyalty, and determination. Now earning $110,000 per year (nearly $1.4 million today), Dorothy was affectionately called "Fifth Avenue's First Lady."

With Dorothy at the helm, Lord & Taylor continued to grow. In addition to opening more branches, Dorothy introduced new services, including personalized in-store shopping and over-the-phone shopping, with trained store employees who would help customers shop. She also divided the department store into small, boutique-like shops that specialized in areas such as sportswear, accessories, bridal wear, petite sizes, and maternity clothing.

In 1946 and 1947, Dorothy earned numerous achievement awards, including an "Outstanding Women in Business" award through the Associated Press. She headed the American Red Cross in 1949 and launched the famous "American Look" clothing line – sportswear with a twist of elegance, comfort, and style. She also oversaw the development of a special line of clothing for teenagers, thereby capturing a whole new market.

Driven and focused on her career, Dorothy remained single. The fact that she cultivated business relationships with male executives in New York City suggests that she was not isolated or cut off as one of the few women in the corporate world. Indeed, Dorothy Shaver saw fashion as the path to growth, stability, and recognition.

In 1958, Dorothy's health began to fail. She died in June 1959, just before her 66th birthday. During her lifetime, Dorothy believed women should have the same opportunities as men, even though, at that time, they truly did not. She was one of the very few who successfully climbed the corporate ladder and became a leader in business.

Dorothy's gracious generosity of spirit helped build a solid American fashion industry that was celebrated by a wide range of designers, manufacturers, and store managers. Her groundbreaking ideas and tireless determination continue to inspire retail entrepreneurs today.

Dame Anita Roddick

1942 - 2007

A troop of howler monkeys signals dawn with a deep, bellowing chorus. A man treads lightly on the spongy forest floor. He stoops down and examines a melon-sized fruit. Satisfied, he tosses it into his hand-woven basket. Later, back in his village, family members help remove the soft flesh, crack open the nuts, and collect the many seeds.

Recently, outsiders have offered cash in exchange for trees – lots of trees. Village elders say companies plan to clear-cut this land along the Xingu [shin-goo] River in Brazil. The Kayapó [kahy-a-poh] people fear this will leave them with few resources to pass on to their children. Without trees, their land is worthless.

The year is 1990. Into a remote rain-forest community enters entrepreneur Anita Roddick. She wants to help the Kayapó people put a stop to the clear-cutting of rain-forest lands. Together they find an answer in the sweet-smelling oil that comes from the towering Brazil nut tree. The nuts contain oil that is rich with vitamins. What's more, the oil makes a nourishing ingredient in personal-care products – Anita's domain. After some difficult negotiating, the Kayapó and Anita come to an understanding. Anita agrees to buy this special oil from the Kayapó people. She will feature it in her new hair-care product, Brazil Nut Conditioner.

Anita Lucia Perella was born in a dimly lit bomb shelter on October 23, 1942, in the middle of the Second World War. Her mother sought refuge there during an air raid on Littlehampton, England, a town south of London. When the sirens stopped and the family emerged above ground, the coastal town was still.

Anita's parents, Gilda and Donny, were Jewish-Italian immigrants. They lived in a working-class neighborhood and were the first Italians to move to the area. Because of this, Anita remembers they often felt like outsiders. Her family played loud music, spoke Italian, and often shouted at each other. While her friends' families ate such foods as fish and chips or beans on toast, Anita's family devoured big bowls of flavorful pasta with tomato sauce and lots of garlic.

Anita's parents ran a restaurant called the Clifton Café, and her mom was the cook. Her grandmother liked to help by peeling potatoes in the back garden. After school and on holidays, Anita was expected to work, too. She and her siblings had to bring in coal for the fireplace, clean out the grates, take customers' orders, make change, clear tables, wash dishes, butter bread, and do the shopping. Anita became used to hard work.

At age eight, Anita faced family upheaval. Her parents divorced. Then, her uncle Henry, Donny's first cousin, bought the café and moved in with Anita's mother and the children. (Henry was in love with Gilda.) Henry, who had been living in the United States for several years, converted the café into a trendy American-style diner. It had a long,

Three Quotes

Three heroes inspired Anita with their words.

- "Only the gentle ever get really strong." – James Dean, a 1950s movie star

- "One life is all we have and we live it as we believe in living it. But to sacrifice what you are and to live without belief, that is a fate more terrible than dying." – Joan of Arc, the girl who led an army

- "Love the earth and sun and the animals…" – Walt Whitman, an American poet

shiny bar and high bar stools. They served ice-cream sundaes and Coca-Cola. Gilda purchased a Wurlitzer jukebox for the diner. It played all the latest rock 'n' roll tunes, and the diner was a favorite spot for teenagers.

When Anita was nine, Donny died. Soon after, Gilda and her true love, Henry, were wed. He predicted that Anita would go on to "do great things," but he didn't live to see this happen. Eighteen months after the marriage ceremony, Henry died of tuberculosis. From then on, Gilda ran the diner with lots of help from her children.

Working and going to school left Anita with little free time. Her teachers encouraged her to read, and this introduced her to new ideas. At age 10, she came across a life-changing book about the Holocaust. The book made her angry. How could people have let those horrible events happen? Anita vowed that she would stand up and shout against injustices.

When she was about 18, Anita's mother told her some shocking family news. Donny was not her real father, Henry was. Gilda explained that she and Henry had been involved in a secret romantic affair when Anita's older sisters were very young. This news was upsetting and life changing, but Anita was strong and mature enough to accept the news and move forward.

Before long, Anita had to start making decisions about her future. She was offered a spot at a drama school, which seemed exciting, but her mother didn't like the idea of her daughter becoming an actress. Anita didn't want to be a nurse or a secretary, so she settled, at last, on being a teacher. While studying, an educator at Newton Park College of Education taught Anita the importance of aesthetics – the way artistry, design, and color bring about a desired effect. Anita began to develop her own "eye" for beauty.

In 1962, Anita earned a three-month scholarship to study in Israel. This rewarding opportunity sparked a life-long love for exploring and adventure. Then, a junior school in England hired Anita to teach. But instead of going straight back to England, Anita took a side trip to Paris and worked for a newspaper. She enjoyed this job so much that she turned down the job offer at home and stayed on with the newspaper for nearly a year.

When she returned to England and got back to teaching, Anita felt restless and wanted to see more of the world. She collected her savings and set off again. She backpacked around Europe before taking a job researching women's rights. After a year, free-spirited Anita resigned from her job and embarked on a trip around the world, visiting the South Pacific, Australia, and parts of Africa. While traveling, she became interested in learning from groups of local women in small communities. She chatted with them and collected information on skin-care rituals. She was intrigued with the natural ingredients they used, such as cocoa butter, aloe, and coconut. The women had fabulous skin and shiny, healthy-looking hair. Anita started to rethink conventional personal-care products and tried out some of the women's rituals. She even tried washing her hair in mud!

Back in Littlehampton, Anita's homecoming celebrations with her mother included meeting Gordon Roddick, a farmer, poet, and explorer. Gordon's Scottish father worked in finance as a broker buying and selling grain. Gordon, however, had a more adventurous streak. He had already worked in Africa and canoed down the Amazon. Somehow, Gilda was convinced the two 26-year-olds would make a perfect match, and she was right. Anita was petite, with wild curly hair, long, flowing skirts, and lots of energy and attitude. Gordon was fearless, tall, and handsome and sported a beard. The pair fell in love instantly, and – after just four days of talking – Anita impulsively moved in to Gordon's flat. Anita went back to teaching for a short time, but by then, her sights were set on becoming a mom. The happy couple had their first child, Justine, in 1969. During a trip to the United States to visit friends in San Francisco, they decided to get married – in the glitzy city of Reno, Nevada. Then, back in England, in 1971, they celebrated the birth of their second daughter, Samantha.

With two young children, Anita and Gordon thought they should settle down and earn a living. Anita wasn't keen on teaching. Instead, the young couple, modeling themselves in part after Gilda, tried their luck at being entrepreneurs in the hospitality and restaurant industries. They opened a bed-and-breakfast hotel and then a restaurant. They cooked and cleaned nonstop, but they also became very interested in local politics and social issues. They delighted in posting bold questions about hot topics on their windows to spark debate and stir their customers to take action.

Then, out of the blue, Gordon told Anita he wanted to pursue a two-year solo journey on horseback through South America. He was inspired by the journey of a famous Swiss explorer who traveled alone on horseback from Buenos Aires, Argentina, to New York City – more than 10,000 miles (16,000 kilometers). Anita agreed readily, but realized she'd have to find a new, more manageable way to support her young family while Gordon was away.

First off, she needed a business plan. Inspired by the Indigenous women's skin-care knowledge and use of natural ingredients – and also by a natural skin-care store in Berkeley, California – Anita set to work. Swiftly, her plan began to blossom. She'd always been interested in the cleansing, moisturizing, and anti-bacterial properties of natural ingredients, so this seemed like a good fit. She decided to open a small shop featuring personal-care products. Anita met with an herbalist, and together they created several recipes for sweet-smelling lotions, shampoos, and soaps. Then, Anita got to work mixing up concoctions in her garage, including cocoa-butter moisturizer and tea-tree facial oil.

The bank denied her request for a loan to launch her company, but when she sent Gordon – a man in a suit – to meet with the bank manager, the business received a loan of £4000 (about $12,000) in start-up money. Anita was perturbed by this experience, but took the money and focused on searching for a suitable shop to rent in Brighton. A grubby store on a small street that housed two funeral homes had great potential, so Anita signed the lease and received the keys. The first task was to paint the dingy walls dark green to cover the damp blotches that were stained with mold.

Thinking back to what she'd learned about aesthetics, Anita commissioned an art student to design a store logo and product labels. Then, Anita painted a sign with gold leaf letters to hang above the store window. The charming shop was coming together nicely, but she needed bottles to hold her lotions and shampoos. She went to a local hospital and bought plastic bottles designed to hold urine samples. This was enough to fill her shelves, but no more. Next, Anita had friends help her fill bottles, affix neat labels, and set up attractive displays. Altogether, the green paint, handwritten labels, fruity scents, and market-stall look created a unique and attractive identity for her small store. The Body Shop opened its doors in March 1976.

At first, Anita's close friends dropped in to see the shop and try her products. Gradually word spread, and eager new customers came to see what the fuss was about. Happy customers left with their distinctive bottles of Body Shop products. More and more bottles were leaving the shop, which should have been good news, but this actually created a problem. Anita didn't have enough money to buy more bottles. Then, she had a great – and very simple – idea. She'd give customers a discount if they returned used bottles for a refill. This idea came straight from her mother's recycling habits during the war years, when she'd been struggling to feed the family. Gilda's resourceful methods would help Anita's business stay afloat. What's more, this refilling practice would encourage customer loyalty and help her cash-flow problem. Indeed, the environmental benefits were not on Anita's mind in those early days. It was a lack of finances that prompted her to set this business practice into motion. Her friends and customers, who had a liking for wholesome and natural products, readily embraced her clever recycling initiative. Later, as environment-friendly practices gained momentum and awareness spread, Anita was honored as one of the world leaders in this area. After all, The Body Shop products were not over-packaged, and they encouraged customers to refill their containers. Six months later, business was thriving, and Anita was able to open a second shop.

Gordon had completed 2,000 miles (3,219 kilometers) of the epic journey when his horse collapsed. He called off the remainder of his trip and returned home to his family.

Going...
Going - Public!

When a small business grows and becomes increasingly successful, the next natural step is to "go public." The owners invite shareholders to invest in the company. In this way, the owners give up much of their control, "passing the reins" to the shareholders or investors. The investments are small parcels of ownership called "shares." Share prices can change as the company becomes more, or less, profitable. Shareholders want their shares to increase in price so that, if they wish, they can sell their shares at this higher price and earn a profit. Going public puts a lot of emphasis on profits.

By then, business was booming. Anita's wares now included a range of 15 different products. Gordon was impressed and very proud of his wife's accomplishments. The Body Shop was no longer struggling. It was gaining momentum, and Anita was excited about the possibilities. She told Gordon that she had many other ideas. Gordon teamed up with her enthusiastically, taking charge of finances and legal issues, which were more his strengths. Anita continued to focus on developing new products, overseeing design, and spearheading public-relations initiatives. Together, the pair forged ahead. The future looked very bright.

Anita's reasons for going public included securing better locations in upscale commercial neighborhoods for her stores. This would position The Body Shop closer to upscale boutiques. The company would have more money to invest in Anita's social and political campaigns. On the day the company went public in April 1984, The Body Shop shares started at 95 pence per share. By the end of the day, the price had nearly doubled. The shareholders who had purchased shares in the morning were very happy indeed. In the span of one day, Anita became a millionaire. Her company was now worth £8 million (nearly $11 million) and boasted 138 stores.

Less than eight years after launching her shop, unconventional Anita – with her rebellious, punk-rock-inspired Doc Marten boots and unruly hair – was declared Business Woman of the Year. With this award came lots of public recognition from her peers. For

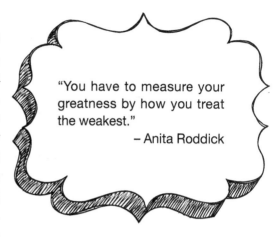

"You have to measure your greatness by how you treat the weakest."

– Anita Roddick

years she'd been bucking the trends and conducting business on her unique model. She had always cited love, education, and empowerment as the foundations of The Body Shop. This was in sharp contrast to big-business's conservative ideals of sales, profits, and price. In spite of her alternative approaches, by 1985, at age 43, she was the fourth-richest woman in the United Kingdom. People then began to ask: Had Anita compromised her morals and sold out?

Anita swore her business wasn't all about profits. In fact, it wasn't even about wholesome personal-care and cosmetic products. For her, The Body Shop was a way to prove to the world that it was possible to run a business based on good ethics. Even more importantly, the business with all its franchises represented a way to communicate with the world. Anita viewed her stores as a means of raising awareness about humanitarian issues, social justice, and the environment. Body Shop posters promoted the natural ingredients of the company's products and connected customers with stories of real farmers living in developing communities. By purchasing ingredients from small communities in poor countries, Anita felt she could help bring about positive change. For example, an in-store poster for Body Butter that promotes community trade explains, "From Ghana our shea butter gives women the opportunity for business training in a male dominated society."

On her company's website, Anita posted the statement, "Businesses have the power to do good." On the sides of Body Shop trucks, used to transport products to stores, she eagerly posted thought-provoking political messages, not advertisements. The slogans and images made people question their views on issues from animal rights, to women's bodies, to protecting the planet. The messages were strong and edgy – sometimes angry. It was all about raising a stir and getting people thinking, talking, and changing.

Anita and Gordon Roddick promoted human rights and environmental causes. They expected Body Shop franchise owners to share their passion.

Anita set out firm rules for owning a Body Shop franchise. The owners must demonstrate that they are involved in community issues and support good causes. Store owners must be committed to The Body Shop values, which Anita

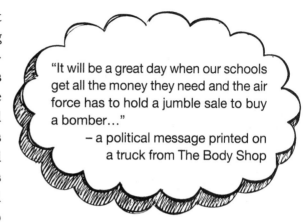

"It will be a great day when our schools get all the money they need and the air force has to hold a jumble sale to buy a bomber..."
– a political message printed on a truck from The Body Shop

outlined in detail. Accordingly, they must also oppose animal testing, support community trade, stand up for human rights, promote a positive body image, and protect the health of the planet. Inside each store, these same values were evident and bold. From the posters on the walls to the brochures on the counters, a visit to The Body Shop kept concerned customers up-to-date with world issues and humanitarian causes.

For Anita, The Body Shop was a vehicle to share information. She began to campaign tirelessly to stop the destruction of rain-forest lands. She had beautifully designed, high-impact posters displayed in all her shops. Then, she supplied her customers with more facts about the rain forest. Next, she defended the rights of Indigenous People who make the rain forest their home. The campaign took several years, but her approach was effective.

In 1988, Anita discovered that ranchers had set a huge swath of rain-forest land on fire. She was outraged and immediately sprung to action. In all, she collected more than a million letters of protest through The Body Shop and her customers. She and many supporters hand-delivered the letters to the president of Brazil, asking him to stop the burning. Heaps of media attention worked in their favor and furthered

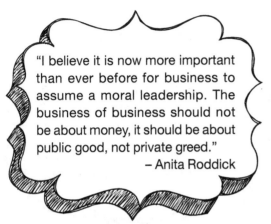

"I believe it is now more important than ever before for business to assume a moral leadership. The business of business should not be about money, it should be about public good, not private greed."
– Anita Roddick

the cause. The Brazilian government made new laws that limited cutting or burning trees in the rain forest. This issue shows how people like Anita can exert power on a government and bring about positive change.

Inside the company, however, the changes were not so positive. After The Body Shop opened stores in the United States, sales began to decline. Other shops started selling natural-ingredient personal-care products for less money and competed for the same customers. The main difference, Anita noted, was that they copied the products of The Body Shop, but not the ethics. Another obstacle was that American shopping malls had strict rules about the kinds of posters that could be hung in mall stores. Mall managers said "no" to many of the edgy, campaign-based posters that were standard fare for The Body Shop. Customers came to The Body Shop wanting refills for containers from competitors. It was confusing!

In 1994, Anita paid for store advertising for the first time. This marked a big change in corporate policy. By the late 1990s, Anita agreed to restructuring. Patrick Gournay became the chief executive officer (CEO), with Anita and Gordon as co-chairs. Then, in 2002, the Roddicks stepped down, becoming directors, but no longer executives. At this point, Anita sadly declared that her business had "lost its soul." She was not happy with its profit-driven direction. In the meantime, critics accused Anita of being a fraud. People started questioning the ethics of the company. Anita and Gordon were forced to go into damage-control mode to defend the reputation of their business. Things were getting ugly. In the meantime, The Body

Shop had continued to grow; there were more than 2,000 stores around the world.

Problems went from bad to worse when Anita faced illness and became acutely aware of her own mortality. In 2004, her doctors said she had a diseased liver. This condition was linked to her catching hepatitis C, a dangerous disease, 30 years earlier. Anita's failing health only made her campaign harder and work faster.

In 2006, Anita sold The Body Shop to L'Oréal, a cosmetic company based in France. This news received huge amounts of criticism, even from her loyal customers and supporters. Anita firmly believed that The Body Shop team, which would operate independently from L'Oréal, would help influence the cosmetic giant to change some of its policies and become more committed to ethical issues, such as community trade. While

Eugene Skeef with Anita Roddick during the official opening of the Blind School she funded in Sarajevo, Bosnia.

L'Oréal agreed to stop testing cosmetics on animals in 1993, they continued to use animal testing for ingredients in their products. But Anita's initial hunch was correct. L'Oréal has been investing in chemical tests (an alternative to animal testing), and in 2012, L'Oréal was deemed one of the World's Most Ethical Companies. Now that's good news!

The sale left Anita with enough money to focus solely on her campaigning and charities. Sadly, she didn't have much time to do this. Anita died suddenly, surrounded by her family, at age 64 on September 10th, 2007. In her full and rich life, Anita found tremendous joy in spurring people to take action to bring about widespread social and environmental change. Her extraordinary bravery allowed her to challenge traditional business practices to help the weak and oppressed. Perhaps her most inspiring message to young people is her famous quotation: "Do something. Anything." Certainly, the legacy Anita Roddick has left will inspire others to do good work through business.

India's Deal-Maker
Naina Lal Kidwai

1957 -

Nine-year-old Naina sprints over to her father's chair and hops up. Stretching her long, slender legs so that her toes graze the floor, she pushes off and sends the chair spinning around in a tight circle. The young girl extends her feet straight out in front and lets the dizzying motion slow. Gradually the chair comes to a halt. Pressing back into the cushiony fabric and running her hands along the arm rests, she surveys the expansive view from her father's office window. She turns away from the window, allowing her eyes to fall on the large oak desk and takes a quick inventory of the items neatly arranged on the shiny surface: phone, notepad, pens, desk calendar, newspaper.

Naina loves visiting her dad's office. The professional atmosphere seems to demand a deep respect. Maybe this is the kind of place where she would enjoy working. Already, Naina knows she'll want to find the type of job where she can make a difference.

Naina Lal was born into a traditional Hindu family (with some Sikh ancestors) in the north Indian town of Kolkata. Her father, Surendra Lal, was an executive in an insurance company. Her mother came from a family of "industrialists," or entrepreneurs and executives who work in manufacturing businesses, such as steel, textiles, oil, and paper products. Naina's mother's brother – Naina's uncle – was a well-known industrialist who headed Ballarpur Industries Limited. Naina grew up in Mumbai (formerly Bombay), Shimla, and Delhi, India.

As an elementary-school girl, Naina received top grades. Even at a young age, she was self-motivated to work hard and strive for excellence. "I was fairly good with numbers," she recalls. Her talents also extended to sports, and she enjoyed being part of a team. Naina used to compete for her school in every form of athletics that was offered. There's no denying she was an accomplished all-round student.

Naina and her sister, Nonita, went to an elite boarding school called Loreto Convent, Tara Hall, in the charming northern "hill town" of Shimla. Sister Cyril – an enthusiastic, energetic, and nurturing teacher at the school – inspired Naina and taught her "the art of positivity." During her high school years, she was always first in her class in every subject. Naina often held leadership roles and became Head Girl in her senior year. Throughout high school, Naina joined many sports teams and clubs, including basketball, badminton, drama, and the library squad. Her greatest passion, besides athletics, was the debate team. Researching a topic and arguing from a certain point of view came naturally to Naina. She argued passionately and persuasively about many different causes and learned not to lose her cool while doing so. Debating helped Naina develop her ability to think quickly and clearly while under pressure. It also taught her to become an exceptional communicator. Critical thinking skills, communication skills, and

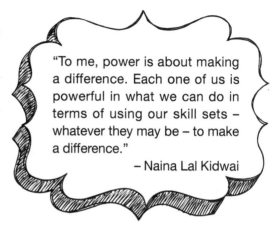

"To me, power is about making a difference. Each one of us is powerful in what we can do in terms of using our skill sets – whatever they may be – to make a difference."

– Naina Lal Kidwai

teamwork would serve her well in the workplace. Evidently, Naina was already thinking about her future; for, at age 16, she made it known that she wished to pursue a career in business. Few women held executive positions at that time in India, or in Western countries, but Naina was convinced that she was heading for a job in an executive suite. She wanted to make deals with big players in the world of high finance. Discussing ideas around a boardroom table was very appealing to her.

After graduating from high school, Naina studied economics at Lady Shri Ram College for Women, University of Delhi. Her schedule – going to lectures, studying, and doing homework – left her with lots of free time. Naina liked to be really busy, so she looked for something stimulating to occupy her time. She became active in student politics, was well-supported by many students, and, at the end of her first year, she was elected president of the student union. This involvement kept boredom away and helped Naina continue to fine-tune her negotiation skills and her public speaking skills – in both English and Hindi. Sometimes she stood up on tables in the canteen (lunch room) and gave lively speeches. Including the line "President of Student Union" on her resume was guaranteed to impress future employers. Without question, Naina was building up a powerful skill set that would make her credentials stand out.

Enthusiastic about seeking further education, she talked to her parents about doing a Masters of Business Administration (MBA) at a foreign university. Her extended family was shocked by this notion, but her open-minded parents consented, with one major condition: Naina had to be accepted into one of the top three colleges in the United States.

In the meantime, after some gentle coaxing by her father, she enrolled in a chartered accountancy course. This would give her more knowledge in the area of finance. (Naina graduated from this program a few years later in 1980.) At the same time, Naina wanted to start working. She approached a well-established firm called Price Waterhouse that provides business advice to companies regarding investments, growth, finances, and taxes. She submitted her application, but was told, "We've never had women here." This didn't stop Naina, who said she "pushed and forced through every connection" until finally they interviewed her. Next, she faced a long period of silence. Then, two months later, Naina recalled a Price Waterhouse executive admitting to her, "You have all the right qualifications." Naina wouldn't take no for an answer. She explained, "I just persisted. I think I must have called every week and said, 'You know, this is absolutely ridiculous. You've got to rethink it.' And they did. They said they were looking at it."

Indian filmmaker Mira Nair (1957 –) is a close friend of Naina. The two went to boarding school together and are among the star alumni at the Loreto Convent. At 19, trailblazing Mira left India to earn an undergraduate degree at Harvard, perhaps putting the idea into Naina's head and helping her friend see that it was possible. Later, when Mira made the movie *Monsoon Wedding* (2001), Naina's children, Rumaan and Kemaya, were cast in roles. Mira is also famous for directing *Salaam Bombay!* (1988), *Mississippi Masala* (1991), and *Vanity Fair* (2004).

In the end, Price Waterhouse hired three women in 1977; Naina was one of them. She was hired as a trainee to start. Before long, she advanced to independent auditor, a position that required examining records of various clients to make sure business had been conducted honestly and correctly, upholding the very best standards. She stayed at Price Waterhouse for three years. Sometime during her final year there, she received acceptance to Harvard. Her future was looking bright.

Naina packed her bags and moved to Cambridge, Massachusetts, to begin an MBA degree from the esteemed Harvard Business School. "It was a very stressful sort of course. I loved it because it sort of packed the day with a huge amount of activity." Naina treasured "the excitement of being in the States, the excitement of being with a very bright bunch of people." She also recalls that "the interaction" and "the new friends, made for a lot of fun." Naina enjoyed the hands-on approach to learning, with students working on real-world case studies and participating actively. Studying at Harvard was, without a doubt, an enriching and exciting time for Naina. Amazingly, Naina was the first Indian student to graduate from the esteemed Harvard Business School.

Upon graduation in 1982, American corporations were interested in hiring Naina, but she was committed to returning to India. Back at home, reunited with her family, she approached her job search carefully and systematically. She would meet with representatives from a number of Indian companies before deciding which one would be the best fit for her. In the meantime,

"I come from a family where women don't work, so I had to fight – really fight! – to go to Harvard."

– Naina Lal Kidwai

Booming Business

India began undergoing major changes in business from 1991 onward. It opened up to more commerce and investment with international companies. There was an explosion of technological products, IT services, and telecommunications. The result of all these changes was that the economy improved significantly.

she already had firm offers to consider. Business leaders were taking note of this well-educated, highly skilled, and very promising young woman. They wanted her to join their team.

In 1982, at age 25, the new graduate accepted a position as an investment banker at the largest foreign investment bank at the time – Grindlays Bank (now called Standard Chartered Bank). From there, she advanced to retail banking, where she held the title Head of Western India. Then she took up various executive positions that spanned the years 1989 to 1994.

Grindlays was a big player in high finance in India at that time, and Naina's experiences were enriching. Perhaps her biggest challenge, however, was her young age. Naina rose up the corporate ladder quickly and was soon managing men and women who were much older than she was. She recalled that "people are watching where you might slip up" and that she "found it difficult to talk to older people as their boss," coming from a culture that holds such deep respect for its elders.

From 1994 to 2002, Naina worked at Morgan Stanley India. The company was renamed JM Morgan Stanley, and under this new name Naina was employed as vice chairman and head of Investment Banking. Colleagues say this was when Naina really proved herself as a dynamic player on the stage of high finance. She excelled at building relationships with clients, forging joint ventures, acquiring new accounts, and closing deals. In 2000, *Fortune* magazine declared Naina the third most powerful businesswoman in Asia. This accomplished, high-finance entrepreneur – now in her mid-40s – was one to watch!

In 2002, she joined the Hongkong and Shanghai Banking Corp. Ltd. (HSBC) as vice chairman and managing director of HSBC Securities and Capital Markets India. After sev-

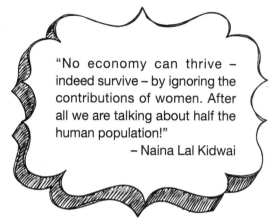

"No economy can thrive – indeed survive – by ignoring the contributions of women. After all we are talking about half the human population!"

– Naina Lal Kidwai

eral promotions, including to head of Investment Banking, she rose to chief executive officer (CEO). *Time* magazine listed Naina as "one of the world's top 'business influentials.'" In 2003, others believed her to be the highest paid banker in India.

Naina describes her field as a "very creative end of finance." She assists large companies with money-related issues, but her role is not fixed on crunching numbers. It's true that Naina acts as a consultant, but she doesn't just give advice. She helps companies grow through making strategic investments, merging with another company, or selling off portions of their assets. Naina is always looking at the big picture, and she must be knowledgeable of international markets. It's a complicated field that requires Naina to constantly analyze financial markets and stay on top of trends and changes.

She advanced to group general manager and CEO of the banking unit. Then, effective April 15, 2009, she was promoted to group general manager and country head HSBC India. At the time, she explained, "My job will involve broader insight of multiple entities and representing India to the global shareholders and investors." Naina was in her early 50s and at the prime of her much-celebrated career.

A few years ago, when she was asked about her management style, Naina replied, "If I were to talk about the traits that I respect most, it is to always be fair and to respect every person's point of view – from the most junior to the most senior employee, man or woman. It is this diversity of ideas and opinions that enriches our decisions." Her colleague, Ravi Menon, said, "The amazing thing about Naina is that everyone feels comfortable approaching her with any problem – personal and professional." Certainly, Naina's passion for her high-finance career is the driving force behind her stellar achievements. Naina is quick to attribute her positive energy to the team of people around her. She says it's important to be surrounded by "can do" people and not to shy away from risks: "Your success ratio, if you are dynamic, should be in the region of 80 to 90 percent so that you are open to change." In other words, some failure (10 to 20 percent) is a necessary part of professional

Naina, as President of the Federation of Indian Chambers of Commerce speaks with Cabinet Minister Anand Sharma in June, 2012.

growth. Learning to achieve goals "without buckling under failures" is something Naina cites as key to success. This approach rings true with many successful entrepreneurs. Risk-takers have the courage they need to propel their businesses forward.

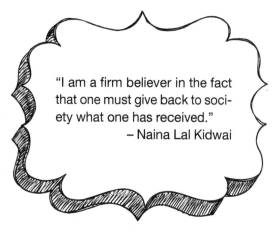

"I am a firm believer in the fact that one must give back to society what one has received."
– Naina Lal Kidwai

In Naina's personal life, she has had to make sacrifices. Married to Rashid Kidwai and mother to son Rumaan and daughter Kemaya, Naina is grateful that her family understands the demands of her work. Today, Rumaan is a filmmaker and Kemaya attends Yale University in New Haven, Connecticut. When her children were growing up, though, it wasn't unusual for Naina to miss birthdays and special occasions due to her hectic work schedule. Even with school-age children, Naina would often wake up at 5:30 in the morning, talk on the phone from 6 until 9:00, go to the office until 8 p.m., and then get back on the phone again until bedtime. Naina didn't grumble about this, however. Instead, she focused on making the most of the time she did share with her loved ones. Often her family would join Naina on business trips, allowing her to combine business with quality family time. The mountains and the jungle are among Naina's favorite regions to visit. She enjoys trekking and being surrounded by nature. Naina's sister, Nonita Lal Qureshi, who is an accomplished professional golfer, explained that even though Naina is fond of classical music, opera, and theater, she rarely has time to pursue these interests. Again, however, Naina looks at the positives. Her hard work has paid off.

Rashid runs a non-government organization called

Grassroot Trading Network for Women and a non-profit organization called Digital Partners. These groups empower women and assist the poor. Already, Naina has contributed to a non-government organization called Self-Employed Women's Association (SEWA) and a rural business school designed for women. As she nears retirement, Naina wants to focus more on assisting enterprising women in rural areas. When women in small villages begin to feel proud of their important contributions in all spheres – from family, to community, to country – the economy will improve and villages will prosper. Naina feels that this is where the changes in women's roles and women's opportunities can have the greatest and most enriching impact. Nevertheless, it is the pioneering efforts of big-city executives like Naina that have made villagers take note. To be sure, villagers now seek advice for their daughters from accomplished role models like Naina. High finance is on the map as a possible career choice for girls. This is a huge change from a generation ago, and certainly Naina assisted tremendously in bringing about this change.

"Self-motivated," "confident," "determined," "honest," "direct," and "dedicated" are all ways in which the investment-banking executive Naina Lal Kidwai has been described. Applauded for being "a shrewd negotiator," Naina quickly became known as a deal-maker – someone who could target clients' needs and close profitable deals within a short time frame. In spite of the fact that there were no female role models for her when she ventured into this field, in India, women are now well-represented in high finance. Indeed, with outstanding people skills and a great sense of intuition, highly skilled women are moving into the coveted corner offices. Nowadays, the dream for a big desk, a swivel chair, and a skyline view is definitely attainable, especially if you dream big, like Naina, and believe in yourself. You *can* do it!

Sheryl Sandberg

1969 -

A well-dressed, self-assured business executive steps into a quiet corner of the conference room, crowded with people. Everyone there is aware of her presence. She's dark-haired, petite, and alluring. She is quick to smile, and when she does, her whole face lights up. Her enthusiasm is infectious. Young men and women nod as they pass by, briefly breaking off their conversations with colleagues. The executive looks down at her compact electronic device and quickly texts: "Smile. Talk into the mic. Good luck."

Sheryl Sandberg, chief operations officer at Facebook, goes out of her way to give junior employees little pep talks, often via electronic messaging. It's important to her to be supportive and to encourage others, especially young women. Sheryl herself remembers, back at university, when she rarely raised her hand in class, in spite of phenomenal grades. Certainly, her old self can relate to a yearning to deflect attention, though these days, it's an impossible task. As second in command at Facebook, Sheryl Sandberg is famous, highly recognizable, and one of the most desired motivational speakers in the country.

Sheryl's pretty sure the young presenter is still anxious, but she's hiding it well. The vocal coaching lessons have paid off. Sheryl can see the junior colleague take a deep breath, relax her shoulders, and steady her hands. She has prepared well, she knows what she needs to say, and she wants to do a good job. That little trace of nervousness will be an advantage to her now. It will bring more enthusiasm and energy to her delivery.

The junior colleague walks calmly to the podium, places her notes on the speaker's stand, sips some water, and begins her rock-solid, dynamic pitch.

Sheryl Kara Sandberg was born in Washington, D.C., but she didn't live there for long. A wealthy Miami, Florida, suburb called North Miami Beach became her home at age two. Her family stayed in this area throughout her years at public school.

Sheryl and her two younger siblings, David and Michelle, enjoyed many fun and enriching opportunities, such as going to Jewish summer camp in Georgia and vacationing in the Caribbean. Sheryl's parents, Adele and Joel, had the means to afford certain privileges. In addition, they were attentive parents who strived to raise their children to be kind, compassionate, and determined. Indeed, throughout their children's formative years, Adele and Joel modeled these values through their own good works.

Years before Sheryl was born, the couple became increasingly concerned about discrimination against Jews living in the Soviet Union. They spoke out and attended public demonstrations. Later, when they had children, it made sense to bring the children along to these peaceful protests. After all – as many social activists know – there is strength in numbers. Sheryl went to her first rally when she was just one year old. This was followed by countless other rallies and participation in letter-writing campaigns. Sheryl's parents taught her to speak out publically for what she believed in. At age 13, Sheryl's photo appeared in a *Miami Herald* newspaper article about her Soviet pen pal and Bat Mitzvah twin, Kira Volvovsky. During Sheryl's Bat Mitzvah ceremony, the rabbi called Kira's name along with Sheryl's. Kira wasn't there, of course, but this "proxy," or token, ceremony for Kira and other oppressed Jews helped spread awareness throughout American Jewish communities and offered kind-hearted support. Sheryl, like her parents, became a passionate spokesperson for this worthy cause.

Sheryl's mother, Adele, gave up pursuing a PhD and teaching French to college students in order to focus on her family. With her free time, Adele devoted a tremendous amount of energy to supporting Soviet Jews and making others aware of the issue. In fact, in 1972, when Sheryl was three years old,

Ongoing Persecution of Soviet Jews after World War II

During the decade after the Holocaust, Jewish people in what was called the Soviet Union continued to endure terrible human rights abuses. (This region now includes 15 post-Soviet states, including Russia, the Ukraine, and Kazakhstan.) Jewish people were killed, arrested, fired from their jobs, and forced to give up their faith. By 1950, two million Jews lived in the Soviet Union. This was the highest population of Jews living in Eastern Europe. From the 1960s up through the 1990s, many of these persecuted Jews fled the Soviet Union and immigrated to other countries, including the United States and Canada.

her mother was one of the founding members of a group called the South Florida Conference on Soviet Jewry. She and Joel worked tirelessly for the American Soviet Jewry Movement for decades. They gave speeches, organized and attended rallies, wrote letters, and even welcomed newly arrived Soviet refugees into their home.

During family vacations to the Caribbean, Sheryl's dad – a high-profile ophthalmologist (eye doctor), researcher, and voluntary professor – used to perform complimentary eye surgery in poor neighborhoods. He also trained local eye doctors, free of charge. With both of her parents committed to volunteering and pushing for social change, it's no wonder Sheryl was determined to find her own way to make a difference in the world.

Friends were important to Sheryl, and she was part of a close group of eight girls – three of whom she met in Highland Oaks Middle School and four of whom she met at North Miami Beach High School. All of her friends came from well-to-do Jewish families. They were studious, hard-working, and ambitious. Although her friends describe teenage Sheryl as an active, sociable, well-adjusted student – and someone bound to succeed – grown-up Sheryl confesses that she "was really a serious geek in high school." In contrast, Sheryl's friend Elise remembers, "We had a good time. We worked hard. We had fun."

On weekends, when she was in high school, Sheryl had her first real job. She worked on Saturday mornings as an office assistant in her dad's office. In this position, Sheryl had to greet customers and record information in the patients' charts. At high school, she led aerobics classes – intensive cardio workouts based on dance moves and accompanied by music. Aerobics was popular during the 1980s; this fitness craze made leg warmers and sweat bands trendy fashion items. Student politics was another area in which Sheryl and three of her close friends participated. Sheryl was elected class president in her "sophomore" (second) year and was on the student government advisory board as a senior. The close friends also enjoyed spending time at each other's houses, going biking, swimming, or shopping. Attending rock concerts was another big highlight in Sheryl's teenage years.

After high school graduation, the girls attended different colleges. To keep in touch, they mailed monthly update letters to each other. Each friend would add a new page with her recent news and then send the ever-growing letter, by post, to the next friend on the list. When a thick envelope arrived at the home of the eighth friend on the list, the letter was seven

Sheryl Sandberg enjoys a good laugh during her talk at the Naval Academy Foreign Affairs Conference in 2011.

pages long and had seven different authors! In the 1990s, when email became a popular communication tool, Sheryl and her friends switched from sending letters or faxes to sending group emails. Nowadays, short updates shared through a private Facebook group allow the friends to keep up-to-date with

Great Minds Crash Alike

Sheryl once crashed the entire Harvard College computer network while crunching numbers for her thesis. Years later, when Mark Zuckerberg (1984 –) attended Harvard, he got in trouble for meddling with Harvard's network while creating a social-networking website called Facemash. This event was depicted as Mark crashing the entire system in a movie called *The Social Network* (2010). Mark left Harvard in 2004 and focused on developing another, now-famous, social-networking platform: Facebook. With this shared connection at Harvard, perhaps Mark and Sheryl were destined to work together.

the simple, everyday happenings in each other's lives. Twenty-six years later, seven of the eight high school friends still see each other regularly.

After graduating ninth in her class with an impressive A++ average (4.646 grade point average), Sheryl headed north to Cambridge, Massachusetts, to study at Harvard College in the fall of 1987. There, she pursued an undergraduate degree in Economics. Along with a fellow student, Sheryl founded an organization at Harvard called Women in Economics and Government. From helping members form study groups to encouraging networking opportunities with faculty and students, this group – which still operates today – supported female students studying in the fields of Economics, Government, or Social Studies. Professor Larry Summers acted as an adviser for Sheryl's final thesis project, and during the process the two formed a solid working relationship. Larry was already impressed with Sheryl's grades, but he soon became aware of her managerial strengths. When Sheryl organized an Economics Association reception, all the details – from accurate name tags to an effective schedule – were perfect. This meant the participants were pleased and the event unfolded as planned, without any double bookings, broken equipment, or food shortages. Larry took note and kept his eye on Sheryl's achievements. Upon graduation from Harvard in 1991, Sheryl was honored with the John H. Williams Prize. She was the top graduating student in Economics.

In 1991, Sheryl's mentor, Larry Summers, left Harvard and accepted a position of Chief Economist for the World Bank (an international financial institution with a goal of reducing poverty). Larry hired new-graduate Sheryl to work as his research assistant for a two-year term. This experience increased Sheryl's awareness of diseases and health conditions that were common in India – the focus of her research tasks.

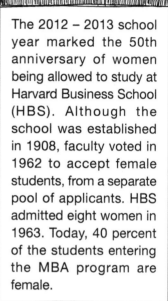

The 2012 – 2013 school year marked the 50th anniversary of women being allowed to study at Harvard Business School (HBS). Although the school was established in 1908, faculty voted in 1962 to accept female students, from a separate pool of applicants. HBS admitted eight women in 1963. Today, 40 percent of the students entering the MBA program are female.

Needless to say, having the World Bank on her resume was a tremendous asset. But rather than seeking a new position and applying her knowledge of economics, Sheryl – who was driven to climb high and make a difference – chose to further her studies. In 1993, she began her Masters of Business Administration (MBA) at Harvard Business School. She graduated two years later, earning the highest distinction, which is an honor awarded to graduates in the top five percent of the class. There was no doubt this young woman had sharp intelligence, and she knew how to use it, with stellar results.

Sheryl rejoined the workforce in 1995 and worked for McKinsey & Company as a management consultant. She conducted research, made recommendations, solved problems, and kept projects on schedule. While working at McKinsey, Sheryl married Brian Kraff, a Washington businessman, in 1996; their marriage ended after about a year. Sheryl's connections to Larry Summers again proved to be rewarding when Larry accepted a position with President Clinton's administration. Larry then called upon Sheryl to be his chief of staff. This exciting position ended when the Democrats lost power in 2000. Thirty-one-year-old Sheryl figured that what was having the biggest effect on people was technology. Wanting to be part of this exciting change, Sheryl moved across the country to Silicon Valley in California – the hub for information technology.

The next stop on Sheryl's career path was Google Inc. She took on the role of business-unit general manager and spearheaded advertisements on websites, helping this giant, multinational company, which creates Internet-based products and services, grow and prosper. In 2004, partway through her seven productive years at Google, Sheryl married David Goldberg, a businessman. Sheryl and David welcomed a son in 2005 and a daughter two years later. Now vice president

Successful Harvard Business School Alumni with Executive Roles

Ann S. Moore, MBA 1978
• Former chairwoman and CEO of Time, Inc.

Meg Whitman, MBA 1979
• Former CEO of eBay; CEO of Hewlett-Packard

Sue Decker, MBA 1986
• Former president of Yahoo! Inc.; entrepreneur-in-residence at HBS

Abigail Johnson, MBA 1988
• President of Fidelity Investments

Jane Fraser, MBA 1994
• CEO of Citi's Global Private Bank

of Global Online Sales and Operations, Sheryl was in the public eye as a high-profile Google executive and mom. Sheryl put social advocacy on Google's agenda in 2004 by launching a branch of the company that focuses on giving back to society. Google.

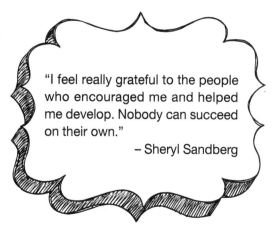

"I feel really grateful to the people who encouraged me and helped me develop. Nobody can succeed on their own."

– Sheryl Sandberg

org develops technologies that positively impact people, such as health care, education, and clean-water initiatives. Sheryl was singled out as the youngest person on *Fortune* magazine's 50 Most Powerful Women of 2007 list.

Multiple nannies, cleaning services, and a husband who does half of the household and parenting tasks allow Sheryl to juggle her roles. When asked about work-life balance, however, Sheryl laughs and concludes, "So there's no such thing as work-life balance. There's work, and there's life, and there's no balance." Instead, she believes in blending work with life, leaving the office at 5:30 p.m. and resuming work in the evening after the kids are in bed.

In December 2007 Sheryl met Mark Zuckerberg, the co-founder and CEO of Facebook, a hugely popular, Internet-based social-networking platform. At the same time, she'd been considering a career move elsewhere, but Mark offered her an executive position, chief operations officer (COO) – or second in command. Sheryl shook hands with Mark on March 2008 and sealed the deal. Since then, it's been full steam ahead.

At Facebook, Sheryl oversees the business side of the company. Her goal was to make Facebook profitable. She focused on bringing in money by placing "discreet" ads on the pages. Advertisers pay for these ads and this earns money

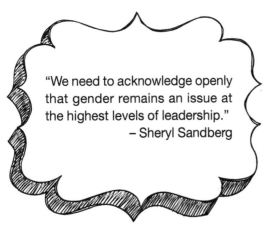

"We need to acknowledge openly that gender remains an issue at the highest levels of leadership."
– Sheryl Sandberg

for Facebook, helping it grow. Two years after Sheryl joined, Facebook was profitable. Three years later, the company had grown to having a staggering "$2 billion dollars in annual revenue" and ten times more people with Facebook accounts. The company was expanding at a rapid-fire pace. Its quick growth may be due, in part, to the work culture that Facebook promotes. On the walls inside the office building, slogan-based posters remind employees to "Move fast and break things" and ask, "What would you do if you weren't afraid?" Clearly, the management at Facebook – and this includes Sheryl – wants the employees to take chances and move forward with confidence and bravery. This type of thinking is essential in a dynamic, innovative, and cutting-edge company like Facebook.

The unconventional business culture doesn't stop with its philosophy. The office has an open, spacious, and industrial look with brightly painted walls, stereo systems, modern furniture, comfy couches, pillows, and artwork. Employees may visit any of the small kitchens found throughout the office and enjoy a free gourmet meal, a quick bite, or a drink, such as a cherry cola. There are ping-pong tables and basketball courts for employees who want some exercise or just need to relieve some stress. To top it off, employees are encouraged to write on the "real" Facebook wall.

Sheryl is a sought-after public speaker who inspires new graduates and encourages young entrepreneurs. She is a strong advocate for increasing the number of women in executive roles. In 2010, she publically expressed her concern that women held just one-fifth of the top executive jobs in the United States. Thoughtful and strategic, Sheryl encourages female junior staff members to sit next to senior executives at conference-room tables, on airplanes, or anywhere else they might have a chance to get acquainted, show off their skills, and make a good impression. It sounds simple, but these steps can help young women gain recognition for their accomplishments – and give them the confidence to strive for high-profile positions.

When Sheryl was finally invited to join Facebook's board of directors in 2012, people were pleased. Previously, Facebook had been under fire for not having any women on their board. (Technology fields are known for having few women, especially on corporate boards.) Clearly, much more progress is required to correct the gender imbalance, but it's a step in the right direction. Sheryl thinks this can happen at Facebook and elsewhere if women "lean in" (don't hold back). To be sure, the message Sheryl wants women to get is simple and direct: "You are awesome." She adds, "Work hard, stick with what you like, and don't let go."

Tech-Savvy Women

Ann Douglas, Canadian (1963 –)
• Member of the Canadian Red Cross Twitter Team; known for her talents in spreading urgent messages using social media platforms to help save lives

Zoe Curnoe, Canadian (1971 –)
• Senior Development Manager at Riot Games, a player-focused game company based in Santa Monica, California; former co-chair of Women in Games, Vancouver

Gina Bianchini, American (1972 –)
• Co-founder and former CEO of an online platform called Ning (launched in 2005) that helps people create customized social networks

Sheryl Sandberg speaks at the World Economic Forum held in Switzerland, 2013.

Sheryl's leadership roles aren't restricted to Facebook. She also holds esteemed positions on the board of directors for The Walt Disney Company, on President Obama's advisory council for jobs, and, formerly, for Starbucks Corporation. She has maintained her passion for non-profit associations by sitting on the board of directors for the Center for Global Development and Women for Women International, among others.

Some have speculated that Sheryl's remarkable career path, coupled with her intelligence, her economic skill, and her deep concern for others, may sky-rocket her right into the role of president of the United States. Certainly, when a woman charges ahead as fearlessly as Sheryl has, the possibilities are enormous – and this daring entrepreneur is still striving, stretching, and strategizing to achieve excellence. Throughout her journey, you can bet she'll be looking out for other young women, guiding, encouraging, and promoting their steady progress. If Sheryl's legacy is to have a hand in leveling the gender balance in top executive positions, she will undeniably have changed the world in a significant way. Now, that's exciting.

The Happiest CEO on the Planet
Sue Chen

1970 -

The Chinese character for chaos hangs on the wall of Sue Chen's office. As chief executive officer (CEO) of Nova Medical Products, she's got a great gig. Corporate offices in Los Angeles and Chicago, 70 employees, and lots and lots of happy customers prove her business is thriving. So what's this about chaos? Sue says, "I live chaotically, but happily chaotic."

Sue Chen has been running her own company for 20 years. She sits on the boards of several non-profit groups, is a Young Presidents' Organization member, networks with businesswomen, advocates for sharks, gives to charities, pursues hobbies, and makes videos. Somehow she also finds time to shop in her beach-side community, keep in shape, listen to classical music, have regular pedicures, go out with friends, and plan faraway vacations. There aren't enough hours in the day for this woman's pursuits, but she makes it work. Sue has exceptional organizational skills, but there are limits to keeping so many details in order. She shrugs at her messy office and the smear of hot sauce spilled on her desk. She admits her life is unbalanced and chaotic, but stresses she's happy – really happy. Helping people with mobility challenges keeps her smiling day after day. "I'm not just running a company," Sue says. "I'm changing the industry and I'm changing America."

Sue's mother, Arlene Chen, carried this passport when the Chen family immigrated to the United States. Sue (right) is next to her older sister, Eva. At that time, children could travel on their mother's or father's passport.

Chen Yue-Chia (陳宜佳) was born in the city of Kaohsiung [gow-shung], Taiwan. Yue-Chia's parents decided to immigrate to the United States when she and her older sister were nearly four and five years old. Nowadays, many immigrants choose to keep their original names, but when Sue arrived, it was more common to pick an American name.

In the summer of 1974, her family arrived in the Bronx, a borough of New York City. Yue-Chia – now called Sue Chen – remembers, "Everyone looked very different, sounded different, and my surroundings were different." Unlike most American kids her age, Sue had never tasted ice cream before. After trying a vanilla cone, she was hooked. "I remember having ice cream and thinking, 'This is the greatest place!' And I wanted to stay."

The Chen family stayed, but in the first four years they moved a lot – to four different cities and four different states. Their first stop was the Bronx. Sue's father, who was a medical doctor, began working as an intern at a hospital there, while he studied at university. Her father had to re-do his residency requirement at an American hospital in order to work as a doctor in the United States. A year later, the family moved to Philadelphia, Pennsylvania, where Dr. Chen (whose American name was Bruce) spent two years completing his residency training at Temple University. Sue's baby sister, Tina, was born in "Philly." That was also when Sue started taking piano lessons. She practiced dutifully to an egg timer, every day, as her parents demanded.

Sisters Sue (left) amd Eva enjoy ice-cream cones in America.

Then, when Sue was seven, the family of five moved to Dublin, Georgia, where Dr. Chen finally began practicing as a doctor. He specialized in physical rehabilitation medicine, helping patients recover from health conditions affecting their mobility. Dr. Chen's next job took eight-year-old Sue and her family to Davie, Florida, a rural town with very few minorities. Sue remembers clearly that "everyone had horses and chickens, and you rode your horse to your friend's house." Sue grew up as a country girl who loved nature and didn't mind picking up bugs.

In grade five, when her elementary school held auditions for a western-themed musical, Sue was determined to be cast in the lead role. "I didn't know what the word *lobbying* meant at the time, but I remember talking to the teacher, and I remember planning this from when I was in fourth grade." Telling the teacher why she thought she should get the lead part, and singing as loudly as she could, made Sue a shoe-in for the prized role.

A year later, Sue set her sights on politics. After learning about the U.S. government in social studies class, she decided she should be the president when she grew up. When she found out that this wasn't possible, because she was born in Taiwan – not in the United States – she was really disappointed. A chat with a supportive teacher helped her see that, in all likelihood, she was still going to do something really important. This ambitious streak has always stayed with Sue.

In 1982, Bruce Chen started a manufacturing company with his brothers in Taiwan. He planned to create orthopedic devices and products that would help people move better. He had a vision to produce medical equipment that was functional, innovative, and good-looking – not the same old, tired-looking gray devices. Working together with family members in Taiwan, Bruce would lend his medical expertise to making devices for this new company – devices such as artificial limbs.

Then, sadly and tragically, shortly after forming this company, Sue's father became very ill from the cancer he'd been fighting for 13 years. This was a really difficult time. Sue, age 13, was going through a rebellious stage. She explained, "My father was dying. He was trying to tell me

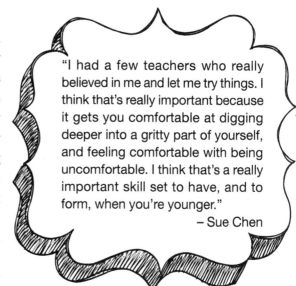

"I had a few teachers who really believed in me and let me try things. I think that's really important because it gets you comfortable at digging deeper into a gritty part of yourself, and feeling comfortable with being uncomfortable. I think that's a really important skill set to have, and to form, when you're younger."

– Sue Chen

all these life lessons in a very short amount of time, and I just didn't want to be told what to do." In spite of the turmoil she endured, Sue is grateful today for some of her dad's "meddling." Sue thought she could get away with choosing whatever courses she liked. When her gravely ill father (who died soon after this) learned Sue hadn't signed up for typing and Spanish, as he'd advised, he was concerned about his daughter's future. He made an appointment with the guidance counselor and changed Sue's courses. Now, years later, Sue sees the value in being a fast typist and thanks her dad for his foresight and his persistence. Typing is a skill she uses every day.

Privately grieving the loss of her father, Sue threw herself into her studies and joined many clubs and teams at Western High School. She earned top marks and kept really busy. She played tennis and took part in a business club offered at her high school. Marketing, merchandizing, and entrepreneurship were areas the club explored. Sue is grateful for the business club, which she describes as her "first entry into understanding entrepreneurship and business." Sue recalls her high school years as being very memorable: "I was very popular. I knew every clique. I had the best high school experience. I wouldn't change it for the world." Sue became president of her graduating class and was voted "Most Likely to Succeed."

Toward the end of grade 12, Sue faced big choices about where to study next. Most of her friends were staying in Florida, but Sue had other ideas. She explained, "I wanted to go to a place where I didn't know a soul." Super-achiever Sue needed some downtime to reflect and grow, in a new place where people wouldn't expect her to be so perfect.

According to her plan, Sue set off for San Antonio, Texas, where she studied at Trinity University. After changing her major a few times, she settled on International Studies with an emphasis on Asian Studies. This program offered Sue an opportunity to explore her roots, culture, and identity. Sue and her sisters had grown up as the only Asian kids at their school. Always trying to blend in, Sue had largely ignored her Asian heritage. Sometimes she felt like she didn't belong in the United States *or* Taiwan. Straddling two cultures was confusing. So rather than focusing on earning top grades, Sue allowed herself room for personal growth. Even though she describes her first few years as "low key," and confesses to not getting too involved in extracurricular activities, the personal rewards were tremendous. Sue concludes, "I came out of it feeling really proud of who I am."

As part of this self-reflective process, Sue realized she loved classical music. This prompted her to pursue a minor in instrumental music. Without her mother encouraging or pressuring her, she began practicing piano again. "It was nice to be able to like it again, on my terms," she said. Yet immersing herself in Mozart, Bach, and Rachmaninoff was just a part of this plan. More than anything, she wanted to face the stage-fright problem she'd developed in high school. So, in her final year, she challenged herself by performing for a large audience. Her hands shook, and she seized up, but it was worth the effort. Sue confided, "It helped me become brave."

> "We're this country that is so defined by mobility. When I came to America, I remember my dad was obsessed with getting a big American car. We had a Chevy Impala. America's all about moving, and going, and cars. Except for when we get older and we have to get another set of wheels, which is a walker."
> – Sue Chen

Academically, she got by, but her years at Trinity were significant in other ways. She established her identity, understood who she was, and became more grounded. In 1992, she graduated with a Bachelor of Arts and then moved to Manhattan Beach, a scenic beach town outside Los Angeles. Then, before Sue could begin a job search, a request came from Taiwan. Her uncles were preparing a joint business venture with a company in California. They knew Sue had taken some law classes at university, and they wanted her to look over the legal documents before they signed the deal. (After the loss of their visionary and medically trained brother, Bruce, they'd been forced to simplify their plan, manufacturing more basic mobility products such as walkers and canes.) Sue read the contract carefully and deemed it one-sided. She strongly advised her uncles to reject it. Her uncles were upset – with her. They were not used to women possessing business knowledge, and they made Sue feel foolish. Frustrated, Sue phoned her grandfather, who respected her opinion and distrusted the Californian businessmen. Her grandfather was a tough man, but he valued family. He suggested Sue start a U.S. company to distribute the mobility products. He was serious.

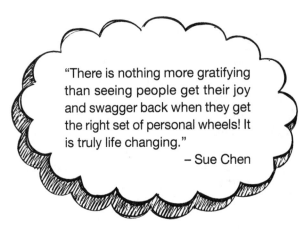

"There is nothing more gratifying than seeing people get their joy and swagger back when they get the right set of personal wheels! It is truly life changing."

– Sue Chen

At 23 years of age, fresh out of university, Sue accepted this offer. The Taiwan manufacturer supplied her with some start-up money and, in 1993, she founded Nova Medical Products in Carson, California, a suburb of Los Angeles. Sue knew very little about the medical product industry when she launched her company, but she was determined to honor her father's vision and prove she could succeed. She was a quick learner and accustomed to striving high and getting results.

Meanwhile, Sue's uncles continued to be skeptical. They figured the U.S. company would last no more than six months. Sue describes her uncles' impression of her this way: "They just didn't think that mentally and physiologically I had the capacity to be able to run a business." In Taiwan, career opportunities for women can be limited. Teaching or secretarial work is most common. Thus, her uncles' attitudes were not unusual. Even though attitudes toward working women have progressed in the United States, the medical product industry is controlled largely by men. Young, petite, attractive Sue Chen would have many challenges ahead.

"I remember early on when I first started, I was listening in on a phone call. One of my competitors was talking about me, and he was laughing a lot: 'Ha, ha! Oh, nice girl, and I'm sure she's very bright, but this company's a joke.'" Sue described the crushing feeling that this patronizing conversation had on her self-esteem. She explained, "Every time I showed up, from then on, at an industry event, I felt like I could hear that." She knew others were aware that she was young, single, and female – that was all true – but it shouldn't be the focus! Like any entrepreneur, Sue wanted to be respected for her business achievements. Her strategy was to work really hard and, when

"I love my company and I love my people. I'm a really fortunate person. I always think I'm the happiest CEO on the planet."
– Sue Chen

working with men, to keep the focus on business. "I made a rule for myself – a law, really – that I would not date anyone in the industry." What's more, when dining with married male colleagues, Sue always invites the businessman's wife. She says this makes for a great business relationship – clearly defined, with no awkwardness.

Sue's foray into business outlasted her uncles' cynical prediction. Six months went by, and then 12. Rather than examining what similar companies were doing, and copying them, Sue followed her instincts. "I did things that were kind of unusual," she admits. For instance, she noticed that competitors didn't print their phone numbers on walkers and other products. This didn't sit right with Sue. "I just thought it was odd, so we put our 1-800 number on the product from the beginning, and we started getting calls from people," Sue explained. "It seemed like such a gift to be able to talk to the people that use your product, and then they would start giving us feedback. A lot of it was really good feedback." With just three employees, Sue often answered the phone. She listened attentively to the feedback and acted on it. As her company became more established and well-known in the area, customers would drop in and request tune-ups for their walkers. Sue became acquainted with people who used walkers. She

Sue Chen is pictured here with Alice, a happy Nova walker user, at a retirement home in the spring of 2011.

met many lovely people with vibrant personalities. This face-to-face contact with customers shattered stereotypes about what walker users were like.

One day, a woman visited the office and greeted Sue. She recalls, "I started chatting with her and all of a sudden I forgot that she used a walker, because she was this super-sassy, amazing, fashionable woman. Then I looked at her walker. 'Oh, right, you use a walker.' Wow, that walker just does not fit her personality at all. And then, that's when I asked her, 'If you could use a walker of any color, what would it be?' She said, 'It would be red, hot red.'" This encounter inspired Sue to launch Voyager, a Ferrari Red four-wheeled walker, in 1995. It was a hit! Nova Medical Products was two years old, and it was already creating innovative, new products. This set Nova apart from the competition and helped

Sue expand her base of happy customers.

After exploring different colors, Sue received customer feedback about the weight of walkers. She contacted the engineers in Taiwan, and they experimented with different materials. Others reported that the seat on the walkers was too small.

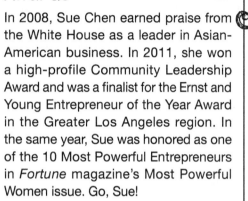

Awards

In 2008, Sue Chen earned praise from the White House as a leader in Asian-American business. In 2011, she won a high-profile Community Leadership Award and was a finalist for the Ernst and Young Entrepreneur of the Year Award in the Greater Los Angeles region. In the same year, Sue was honored as one of the 10 Most Powerful Entrepreneurs in *Fortune* magazine's Most Powerful Women issue. Go, Sue!

In response, Nova created a wider seat, pleasing still more customers. Undoubtedly, Nova customers had great ideas, and Sue was smart. She listened to customer feedback and took action. This made good business sense.

Sue also made it a personal mission to defy stereotypes about people with physical challenges. She summed this up in a 2012 press release to the media: "I want to change the way people face mobility challenges, and [let them] know that life doesn't end just because you need the help of a walker or a wheelchair." From new kid on the block to savvy entrepreneur, Sue was becoming more passionate about her work. Seeing how her products revolutionized people's ability to move was more than emotionally touching – it was addictive! Nova was doing great things. Sue became a strong advocate for walker and cane safety. She chased down people with grubby, cut-open tennis balls on the front legs of their two-wheeled, Medicare-issued walkers and replaced the tennis balls with specially made "walker skis" – at no charge. Sue couldn't get enough of the buzz she got every time she made someone's day. It made her day, too.

As Nova grew, Sue hired more employees. She sought employees who shared her values – people who understood the importance of mobility, respected others, and wanted to make a difference in the world. Sue cultivated an open and friendly atmosphere. Her employees even tried out the mobility products to ensure they really knew them. w with a zippy soundtrack, features Nova employees dancing wildly with pink walkers and canes. As well as promoting breast cancer awareness, the video also blasts away stodgy stereotypes about people with physical challenges.

Sue discovered one way to personalize mobility devices is to offer a range of colors, styles, and patterns for walker "glamour bags," purses, and accessories. This led to the release of floral- and animal-print bags, patterned canes, and creative color descriptors, such as Edgy Aqua, Leopard Diva, and Chocolate Zebra. Some accessories are even made from fun

Sue Chen hams it up in her warehouse,
surrounded by boxes of Nova's mobility products.

fur! Nova's slogan – "As unique as you are" – sure fits with the stylish offerings.

In the spirit of fun and celebration, Nova hosts contests, challenges, and true-to-you walker updates called Mobility Makeovers. Making sure each customer has the correct fit for their walker or cane is essential for safety, comfort, and enjoyment. Next, Chen's team reviews the user's lifestyle and offers good-looking product options that make people proud to be seen with their wheels.

It's true that Sue loves work, but she loves her hobbies, too. In 2004, she took scuba diving lessons and became a certified diver. She delights in traveling to tropical destinations to explore coral reefs and exotic sea life, such as sea anemones and manta rays. With her camera in a waterproof case, Sue takes photos and shoots videos of underwater creatures. Later, she can spend up to a hundred hours editing the video and selecting

Sue is also a conservationist whose passion is saving our oceans and the creatures in it – especially sharks. In scuba gear, she dives with 14-foot tiger shark "Emma" in the waters off the Bahamas. Emma, a celebrity in her own right, has her own Facebook page and is known for being gentle with photographers.

classical background music to put together a stunning memento from her holiday. Sue calls this "dabbling," but her self-taught filming and video-production skills are useful at Nova as well. She often makes videos, featuring her employees and customers. Making videos is a fun, creative outlet for Sue who thrives on being busy.

"I love to dive. And I'm an avid photographer and videographer of sea life. Yet nothing compares to the thrill of knowing that my commitment to Shark Savers and Reef Check is actually helping preserve for future generations the magical and medicinal world of coral and rocky reefs and sharks."
– Sue Chen

Sue is a caring person whose charitable works are far-reaching. Sue's interest in diving led to her passion for saving sharks. She's been on the board of Reef Check since 2008 and active with Shark Savers since 2011. She also donates wheelchairs, walkers, and other medical products to people in developing countries. In her own greater community, too, Sue often spots a need for improved mobility products. For instance, she donated 24 red-and-blue transport chairs (wheelchairs that are pushed by an attendant) to an L.A. music center. Her generosity makes performances accessible to physically challenged individuals who love music as much as she does.

By offering consumers bouquets of canes, purple walkers, and floral-print bags, Sue keeps fun front and center in the pursuit of moving independently and living well. She says, "Doing what is right, and for the greater good, is core to me and my company. Our mission is this: Change the world – everyday – everyway." With her special vision, positive outlook, and bubbly personality, Sue Chen is bound to impact attitudes toward the physically challenged in a profound way.

Sky-High Achiever
Susan Mashibe

1973 -

C ertified pilot Susan Mashibe approaches the Tanzanian government official respectfully. At last an opportunity to voice her concerns! Her hands fly as she passionately describes the aircraft-service business she founded and built herself.

Susan is a courageous and talented business leader who stands out among her peers. She is committed to conducting business in an honest and responsible manner – in spite of the fact that in Tanzania [tan-zuh-NEE-uh] corruption is wide-spread. Many pay bribes to ensure business will run smoothly. Susan is different. She is determined to give the government their fair share so that all Tanzanians will benefit from her company's success. If more businesses act in this manner,

Born third out of six Mashibe children, Susan is a "middle child." Some researchers believe middle children are more relaxed in their manner, but like to be in the spotlight. Susan's middle-child characteristics – her easy-going nature and self-assured attitude – help her shine in business.

Susan believes that her country will eventually become self-sufficient and won't have to rely on foreign aid.

Susan smiles as she talks wistfully about her desire for an electronic payment system in Tanzania. Such a system would make money transfers much easier for her many international clients. Then, looking squarely at the official, she explains confidently, politely, and honestly, "These are the issues I'm facing. I'm really trying to do what's best for this country. But it seems as if I'm not doing the right thing."

The government official has been listening intently throughout Susan's persuasive presentation. He is impressed with the service Susan's business is providing, and he tells her so. Her aviation company is a great boost to Tanzania's economy and will give air access to more people – often very successful business people, esteemed monarchs, and political leaders.

Susan nods and adds that these people will be likely to invest in Tanzania in other ways: spending money at hotels, restaurants, game reserves, and so on. Then, the government official agrees to send a government adviser to Susan's office. Having an expert comb through her records will ensure Susan's business is being conducted properly, in accordance with the law, and in the most ethical, honest way.

"*Asante*" – thank you – replies Susan in Swahili. Her eyes sparkle, and she smiles warmly. This day marks a milestone.

Susan Mashibe was born in 1973 in Kigoma, Tanzania, on the beautiful rocky shores of Lake Tanganyika [tan-gannyee-ka] – the longest lake in Africa and the second deepest lake in the world. At age four, while living in Kigoma [kee-goh-mah], young Susan experienced an emotional incident. She saw her loving parents and siblings fly away in an airplane to Dar es Salaam, the largest city in Tanzania, while she watched with her grandmother. Upset and missing her family, young Susan was "deeply hurt, but didn't cry." Years later, she recounted, "At that point, I decided if I knew how to fly, I would never be left behind again." Dar es Salaam, though not the capital city, was, and is, a center for government administration and business. Since her father was a civil servant, Susan had to endure this feeling of separation far more often than she liked.

Susan spent the rest of her childhood years in Mwanza [mwahn-zah], a lush, green city southwest of the Serengeti National Park, also situated on a lake. The world's second largest lake, Lake Victoria, is often called an inland sea for its mammoth proportions. Known as the "heart of Africa," Lake Victoria connects Tanzania, Kenya, and Uganda. Mwanza is the second largest city in Tanzania by population, with more than two million people (more than the city of Montreal, Canada) – not including the sprawling suburban population.

Susan's passion for airplanes persisted throughout her childhood years. When she was ten, her uncle took her to see the airport in Dar es Salaam. She recalled, "I still remember the feeling that came over me when I saw the British Boeing 737 for the first time. I was speechless. I had never seen something so beautiful and vast, but what fascinated me most was the take-off process." Susan was keen to learn all she could about flying and aircrafts. She continued to dream of becoming a pilot.

Susan attended a public high school in Mwanza. With her interest in flight, Susan's favorite subject was science. It was frustrating, however, because basic equipment, such as Bunsen burners, was lacking. As a result, Susan and her classmates weren't able to conduct experiments or engage in much hands-on learning. Instead, they had to rely on their teacher's explanations or descriptions found in textbooks. This more passive style of learning wasn't ideal, but Susan applied herself fully and achieved good grades.

Upon graduation, Susan was accepted into a teacher training program, a natural choice for a bright, young woman in Tanzania. This was not her dream, however, and she declined. Lucky for her, Susan's parents supported her decision. Mr. Mashibe respected his daughter's desire to become a pilot and was not going to ask her to change her plan. Instead, he encouraged his daughter to study aviation, far away in the United States.

In 1992, at age 19, Susan followed her father's advice and moved to Michigan, where her sister was, too. (She didn't know at that time, but she would stay there, studying and working for ten years!) At first, it was very challenging because everything was so different, from the food to the clothing to the music and local customs. The biggest obstacle was language.

Focus on Mwanza

Known as the "Rock City," Mwanza, Tanzania, boasts huge granite boulders stacked along the lakeshore and in the outlying hills that frame the city. It is a transportation hub, with airstrips, railway lines, and roads. It is jammed with a crush of people and vehicles. Shared taxis (*dala dalas*), cars, small trucks, and bicycles speed through the busy streets. Market stalls and small, one-person shops (*dukas*) sell basic items such as shoes, newspapers, snacks, and groceries, or offer services such as haircuts, phone, and Internet. Street vendors display their wares on a sheet of fabric, spread out on the pavement.

Nevertheless, by 1993, Susan started to take technical courses related to aircraft mechanics at Southwestern Michigan College in the Midwest.

In the summer, Susan worked at Burger King, flipping burgers. This was her first job in the United States, and she "thought it was so fun." No doubt this experience helped Susan improve her English language skills.

Susan continued studying English and taking courses in aviation. Abruptly, in 1995, she received word from home that her parents could no longer afford to support her studies. Susan recalled, "For a moment I thought I was watching as my dream died an inevitable death – I lost hope, and appetite, and as a result got sick."

After visiting a hospital and being advised to go home, Susan returned to Tanzania to restore her health. At that point, Susan "made a lifelong resolve" and vowed, "I would never want to rely on anyone but myself, I was going back to finish my school and would fly on my own."

In 1996, Susan returned to Southwestern Michigan College, wrapped up her aviation courses, and set out to apply her new skills as a trained airframe mechanic. The management at Duncan Aviation in Kalamazoo, Michigan, offered her a job. Susan inspected and repaired turboprop engines on propeller airplanes. She was happy, working hard, and in her element.

Duncan Aviation was a fixed base operator (FBO) – a business, located at an airport, that services aircraft at that airport. The types of facilities and services an FBO may provide include a fuel station for aircraft (like a gas station for cars), a hangar (a large, covered garage where parked aircraft are protected from wind, rain, ice, and snow), an open-air, tie-down area for grounded (parked) aircraft, and mechanical services – from routine tune-ups to repairs. FBOs can also offer flight instruction courses and usually have some facilities for visiting pilots and passengers, such as restrooms, showers, waiting areas, a restaurant, and telephones.

Kalamazoo was also home to Western Michigan University, which offered pilot training. "I started my flying classes at the Western Michigan University," she says. "It was very expensive, and I had to work long hours at night [to be able] to attend class." Duncan Aviation agreed to pay half of Susan's flight school costs, which helped considerably. But finances were not the only obstacle. Not yet fluent in English, Susan struggled to express herself clearly during her flight training course. While the technical skills came quickly, English was hard! Susan had no choice but to persevere. As an aircraft mechanic, pilot, or aviation manager, she would have to be able to communicate clearly in English to the air-traffic-control workers who manage the flow of air traffic and prevent aircraft collisions. Ten years in the United States and lots of hard work led, ultimately, to Susan achieving fluency in English.

Unfortunately, the airline industry was about to suffer a massive decline. On September 11th, 2001, catastrophe struck. Terrorists hijacked four passenger jets and crashed two into the Twin Towers in New York City and one into the Pentagon. The fourth aircraft crash-landed in a field in Pennsylvania. Nearly 3,000 people died and the world was in shock. After this horrible event, new rules were implemented to try to increase passenger safety and prevent this kind of tragedy from recurring. Suspicions were high, and many travelers and airline employees became anxious and slightly paranoid. As for pilots like Susan (not born in the United States), it suddenly became next to impossible to get hired. People were fired; some companies closed. This marked the second major glitch in Susan's efforts to achieve her goal. At this point, she was striving to become a "triple 7 pilot" – a pilot for a Boeing 777 twin-engine jet – and a captain for Delta Airlines. But her student visa, which allowed her to stay in the United States, was expiring. If she didn't get a job offer soon, she wouldn't be able to apply for a work visa. Without the proper papers, she would not be allowed to stay.

In spite of this troubled climate, in 2002, Susan's hard work, passion, and dedication paid off. She became a certified commercial pilot through the Federal Aviation Administration (FAA). Back home, this news made history. Susan had just become the first woman in Tanzania to be licensed as a pilot and aircraft maintenance engineer.

Faced with a downturn in the industry, Susan shifted her thinking. She explained, "I was curious to come back home to see if I could make a difference in Tanzania." She added, "I decided home is where I should be." But Susan was not about to give up on her dream. She was determined to work with

Awesome Aviation Entrepreneurs

Elsie "Queen of the Hurricanes" MacGill, Canada (1905 – 1980)
- First woman in the world to design aircraft; advocate for women's rights

"Although I held many important positions in the aeronautics industry, I am perhaps best known for my work during World War II. As chief engineer for the Canadian Car and Foundry Company I oversaw the production of the Hawker Hurricane in Canada." – Elsie MacGill

Sibongile Sambo, South Africa (1974 –)
- Founder and managing director of SRS (Sibongile Rejoice Sambo) Aviation, a company that offers a wide variety of air services

"For me, managing in an environment that is very male-dominated just comes naturally. It comes from a confidence and willingness to learn, but also from the willingness to make mistakes, learn from them and move on." – Sibongile Sambo

Susan Mashibe overcame financial challenges,
language barriers, and bias against women to become Tanzania's
first licensed female pilot and maintenance engineer.

airplanes. She reviewed her skills carefully and thought about how she could fit into the workforce in Tanzania – and stay in aviation. While she mulled over these ideas, she began to look for work. None of the airports or airlines would hire her. She was overqualified.

At this point, determined Susan knew she had to forge ahead. Why not create her own aviation company – a fixed base operations service, specially created for private, corporate, and diplomatic aircraft flying into Tanzania from abroad? Susan channeled her energy into developing this idea. She used up all of her remaining savings to rent a small office in the Dar es Salaam airport – the same airport where she'd watched those awe-inspiring Boeing 737s as a ten-year-old girl. In 2003, after much hard work, she launched her company, Tanzanite Jet Center – TanJet, for short. "Everyone dismissed my decision, saying I would close up shop after three months," she laughed, "but I am still here."

• The First Inclusive Sagarmatha Women's Expedition Team scaled Mt. Kilimanjaro to its peak in March 2013. The climbers, who used the slogan "educate and empower women," raised awareness about the importance of educating girls

• Rebecca Rees-Evans, a mother of four, from the U.K., holds the woman's world record for the "fastest ascent of Kilimanjaro." She reached the peak's summit in a blizzard on May 21st, 2005. Her time was 13 hours, 16 minutes, and 37 seconds

Her first client was Jacob Zuma, a member of Parliament who would become the president of South Africa. Jacob was so impressed with Susan's handling of his aircraft that she earned the trust of the South African embassy. Before long, she was handling all the private and diplomatic aircrafts coming into Tanzania that were associated with the South African embassy.

"It is magnificent to see what Tanzanian women can achieve today whether in politics, business, or education. As Young Global Leaders, I hope we can inspire and assist more women and youth in Tanzania and Africa to pursue education to the highest levels and fulfill their dreams in life for a sustainable future."
— Susan Mashibe

Today, international pilots applaud TanJet as the "best handler" in Tanzania. Susan's company upholds aviation standards, manages the international paperwork, troubleshoots, and provides guidance and support for the majority of the business jets and U.S. air-force and marine jets that fly into Tanzania. Excellent and reliable service prompts positive feedback, which helps Susan's business thrive. If an aircraft is in need of servicing, Susan and her employees are well-qualified for the job. Being fluent in English helps tremendously in dealing with clients from Australia, the United States, the United Kingdom, and many other countries. Indeed, since January 1, 2008, English has been declared the international language of aviation. Susan is always first on the tarmac, meeting and greeting new arrivals with warmth and courtesy.

Every year, Susan's company pays a staggering half a billion Tanzanian shillings (more than $300,000) in taxes to the Tanzanian government. Unlike most business owners, Susan dutifully and happily pays this sum. With TanJet now employing 25 people, business is thriving, and Susan is eager to play her role in helping other Tanzanians succeed. Paying the taxes she owes is an important part of this.

In 2007, Susan took on a new business asset. She added a giant-size hangar at Kilimanjaro International Airport to TanJet's operations. This hangar, which TanJet leases, has the capacity to store one Boeing 747 (jumbo jet) or three ATR 42s (much smaller, short-haul aircrafts). The hanger was built many years ago but was underused. Susan saw the potential in developing this covered space and never looked back. Out of this vast hangar, Susan reserves about ten percent for her offices. Impressively, the TanJet hangar is the largest aircraft maintenance facility in Africa – and from there Susan has an excellent view of Mount Kilimanjaro, Africa's highest peak.

Susan expanded her business operations by co-founding the Kilimanjaro Aviation Center. Presently, Susan is seeking another investor to establish a repair and maintenance service with her, to serve aircrafts at this location. As founder and executive director of TanJet and the owner of Kilimanjaro Aviation Center, Susan is a busy entrepreneur with lots to juggle.

Once Susan reached 36 years of age, the awards started pouring in. In 2009, she earned an esteemed Archbishop Tutu Fellowship. In the same year, the Tanzania Women of Achievement Awards honored her with the Science and Technology Award. Then, in 2011, Susan was selected from nearly 5,000 candidates to be a Young Global Leader through the World Economic Forum. With clients including foreign ambassadors, politicians, monarchs, top-tier business executives, celebrities, and sergeant majors, TanJet was fast becoming a highly respected company. What's more, it was transforming the way businesspeople traveled by air, not just in Tanzania, but throughout East Africa. TanJet's superior and dependable services made East African travel easier and more accessible.

In the spring of 2011, Susan was honored to participate, as one of 25 young leaders from developing countries, in the Global Women Mentoring Partnership. She was paired with Marissa Mayer, who was then a vice president at Google. Susan "shadowed" Marissa, watching and learning about team management and business strategies for three enriching weeks. "What Marissa taught me is to hire smart people who get things done. I saw how important it was to have a healthy team...You also have to nurture your team well."

Susan's many discussions with Marissa also taught her that giving back to the community is her responsibility as a business owner. Volunteering at community-based schools is both rewarding and enriching for Susan. As a wonderful role model, Susan uses her achievements in business to inspire children to stay in school and work hard. Science education is an area Susan strongly promotes – for girls, especially.

In Tanzania, many parents can't afford the fees to keep their children in secondary school. As a result, the drop-out rate is high. Girls often leave school because they have married (which is allowed when they are as young as 14), they are pregnant, or they've been forced to work. But as Susan knows, children who stay in school longer have better opportunities and may be able to escape the cycle of poverty.

Susan Mashibe is not one to sit back and bask in the glory of her success. Instead, she sees the value in sharing the story of her aviation company – including all the struggles and setbacks – with Tanzanian students. Fully devoted to giving back to society, Susan says, "I just want to inspire young people through my story so they too can go after their dreams and never let anything deter them."

Susan's warmth of character, infectious smile, and positive, never-fail attitude have led to personal success and widespread recognition. For the next generation of aviators, Susan flashes her trademark smile and gushes, "be passionate" and "stay focused." This winning combination of attributes sets young entrepreneurs on an adventure-filled path to success. Dream big and reach for the sky!

Good-News Messenger
Nicole Robertson

1974 -

The experienced media professional steps back, observing the production space with an expert eye. She's looking for anything out of place that's mistakenly crept into view in the filming area. No microphones visible? Check. No cords? Check. No light stands? Check.

At the same time, she listens carefully to the elder who outlines some strategies for supporting Aboriginal youth. This video will showcase Aboriginal achievement for mainstream audiences. It will be used to empower Aboriginal peoples and educate others. She nods approvingly as the elder speaks, exhibiting deep respect and humility.

Nicole Robertson, president of Muskwa Productions, and

her client have been developing this video for several months. Seeing today's filming go so smoothly is a testament to Nicole's experience as a media specialist. Earlier in the process, she met with this client, asked lots of questions, narrowed the focus, and clearly established the target audience. Then, together with the client, she drafted a script, planned locations for scenes, and researched photos to use within the video. Using a special technique, Nicole will pan in on still images, such as historic photos or pictures of students in a classroom, to keep modern viewers, with short attention spans, fully engaged. For now, background music is classified "t.b.a." – to be announced – but she has a few ideas, and you can bet traditional hand drums are high on her list. There will be time for finessing the details later on in the production process.

Nicole's warm, loving family helped Nicole weather the many moves, new friends, and different schools she encountered as a child. Nicole was the youngest, Phyllis the oldest, and Natalie was the middle of the three Robertson girls.

Nicole Robertson describes herself as a Rocky Cree, because her mother's family comes from a historic village called Sandy Bay. The Cree have lived in this area – characterized by exposed rock, pine trees, and fresh water – for thousands of years. (This First Nations

community is in north-
eastern Saskatchewan,
close to the Manitoba
border.) The mighty
Churchill River, which is
found mainly within the
Canadian Shield region,
flows swiftly past Sandy
Bay.

> "The greatest thing I've learned through the years is to know who you are, to understand that, and understand the biggest question, "Who Am I?," and, to believe in yourself, truly."
>
> – Nicole Robertson

Long before Nicole
was born, her grandfa-
ther – or *moshum* – was a highly respected fur trapper and
explorer. Angus Bear delivered mail to remote areas by snow-
shoe, on foot, and by canoe. He had a central role in developing
hydroelectric power in this region. Nicole shares many traits
with her hard-working grandfather, including an entrepre-
neurial nature.

Nicole remembers that when she was young, she began
noticing the differences between her parents and became curious. "Why?" she wanted to know. "What am I?" she asked.
"Who am I?" Her parents helped her begin sorting out these big
questions about her identity. They explained that her father's
family came from Scotland and the Ukraine and that her mother's people are Cree.

Apart from living on a reserve with her mother's family when she was about four, Nicole's family lived in cities.
Sometimes her dad worked as a hospital orderly – a type of
nursing assistant. Other times he was employed as a mechanic,
keeping boiler-room equipment in good repair. Nicole's adventurous mom loved to move, and so her father often changed
jobs. "We lived in every western province across the country
in my childhood," Nicole recalls. Frequent moves meant that
Nicole attended many different schools and got to be really
good at making new friends.

Nicole grew up understanding the English meaning of Cree words such as *mîciso* (eat), *nipa* (sleep), and *mitawe* (play) because her mom speaks fluent Cree (the "th" dialect) and used to say these simple expressions to her daughters every day. Someday, Nicole would like to be fluent in Cree.

In the poor neighborhoods where Nicole lived with her parents and two older sisters, she saw many hardships. Some kids at school didn't have money to buy lunch and hadn't brought packed lunches. Friends would talk about problems at home that sometimes kept them away from school. On blustery days, she noticed people without winter coats and gloves.

In spite of the range of challenges present in her community, Nicole always managed to focus on the positive. For instance, when she lived in Winnipeg, Manitoba, Nicole remembers bicycling home from volleyball practice and stopping at Neechi Foods – a corner store specializing in First Nations foods and products – to buy fries and gravy or freshly baked bannock. Nicole knew she was lucky; she came from a loving family with caring parents who always made sure she had food, proper clothing, and lots of support. Her community may have been a bit rough around the edges, but living close to other Aboriginal youths was a great opportunity. Nicole believes this helped her develop a better sense of her own identity – something that is very important to her.

Getting out of the city and escaping to nature was a favorite pastime for Nicole. Her outgoing personality led to friendships with many Native children who attended her school and lived on First Nations reserves. These friends invited her to attend various organized activities on a reserve, such as a concert for youths. Every summer, she'd visit Sandy Bay and spend time with her cousins "jumping off rocks into a big pool of water," hiking up a rocky hill, or exploring. She also has great memories of going on weekend camping trips with her family.

At school, Nicole liked to write, and so language arts was her favorite subject. Team sports, such as volleyball, basketball, and flag football, gave her a great sense of accomplishment and made her feel like she belonged. She learned to play the flute and liked studying the arts. At home, young Nicole was intrigued by the grown-up world of news and international events. Her parents used to watch an in-depth news program called *The National*. It was on CBC television, usually at 10 o'clock every week night. Nicole, like many children, pleaded with her parents to let her stay up past her bedtime. Occasionally, her parents let her watch this inspiring news program. For most of the 1980s, the show's host was Knowlton Nash, and by age ten or eleven, Nicole knew what she wanted to be when she grew up – a reporter. Determined and single-minded, she never wavered from this dream.

Naturally, young Nicole sought out role models from the Aboriginal community. On television, which later became her favorite medium, there were very few Aboriginal faces. When a public organization called the Canadian Radio-television and Telecommunications Commission (CRTC) launched Aboriginal Peoples Television Network in 1980, faces of Aboriginal newscasters, reporters, and journalists began to appear – and suddenly stories that were meaningful to Aboriginal communities were front and center in the programming. Times were changing!

Unfortunately, the positive changes weren't enough to outweigh some very serious issues occurring in Saskatchewan and across the country in the late 1980s. There was a shockingly high percentage of Aboriginal people in jails, compared to non-Aboriginals. Relations between First Nations and police were very strained. When Nicole was 16, these problems affected her on a personal level. One of her friends, a 17-year-old boy, died.

"He froze to death on the outside of Saskatoon," Nicole relayed solemnly. "It was very heart-wrenching to lose a childhood friend. I realized at the time that there wasn't a lot of justice for Indigenous Peoples in Canada." Many people thought that the teen's death was not an accident. They believed – but the accusations were never proven in a court of law – that her friend was picked up by racist and corrupt police officers. It is alleged that the officers secretly dropped off the youth on a country road in the middle of the night and left him there. But no one was convicted. Nicole, who lost a dear friend, said, "It was very sad." This event "catapulted" her into "wanting to create change."

Aboriginal Women Entrepreneurs to Applaud

Desta Buswa, aspiring business coach, North Spirit Lake First Nation, Ontario
• Participant in a business skills program (Project Beyshick); celebrated for her business plan in 2008

Marie Delorme, founder and president, Imagination Group, Calgary, Alberta
• Launched an art registry that helps Aboriginal artists protect the copyright of their original art

Caroline Marshall, basket-maker, Membertou First Nation, Nova Scotia
• Makes baskets and passes on her skills and knowledge to youth

Becky Qilawaq, filmmaker, Iqaluit, Nunavut
• Depicts the beauty of Inuit culture and promotes positive thinking for youth

Wanda Wuttunee, director, Aboriginal Business Education Program, Winnipeg, Manitoba
• Mentors young women; celebrated as one of Canada's Most Powerful Women in 2011

Nicole praises Saskatoon reporter Betty Ann Adam, who made a difference in Nicole's career path. "She took a bunch of us Native students from high school and we had a weekend in journalism. We stayed in dorms and we got to visit the newspaper, a radio station, and a television station – and we wrote a story!" This experience provided the boost Nicole needed to help her keep her goal on target.

By the time Nicole was 18, she was devoted to educating the public about Aboriginal people. She held fast to her dream of becoming a reporter. The media would be her teaching tool so she could share important stories and raise awareness about Aboriginal issues. With this purpose in mind, she set her sights on post-secondary studies and applied for a student loan. First, she enrolled in an Aboriginal Education Program at Mount Royal University in Calgary, Alberta, to complete some high school credits. Then, she completed a diploma in Broadcasting at Mount Royal. Next, she enrolled in Journalism at Grant MacEwan Community College in Edmonton, Alberta. There, she met Jane Woodward, a faculty member who ran the Native Communications program, and a woman whom Nicole admired greatly.

With her education behind her, Nicole sought out challenging work experiences in order to begin building her media skills. In 1997, Aboriginal producer Lisa Meeches hired 23-year-old Nicole to work in Calgary as a reporter and producer on an A-Channel television series called *The Sharing Circle*, then in its sixth year. (This show went on to become the longest running Aboriginal documentary TV series, concluding after 16 seasons in 2008.) Nicole's six-month experience there served her well. Following this job, the young westerner packed up and moved to Toronto, where she joined Aboriginal Voices Radio. In this position she networked with reporters and editors to gain top-notch media exposure for this radio station serving Aboriginal people in the city.

Muskwa means "bear" in Cree, and Bear is the last name of Nicole's grandfather and mother's family. It is important to Nicole to honor her ancestors. She enjoys collecting bear items to decorate her beautiful home.

A publicity internship at The Banff Centre sent Nicole back to the West in spring 2000. She applied her love of dance to promoting the Aboriginal dance program offered at the center. Creating media packages, writing press releases about upcoming events, and setting up press conferences became her responsibilities.

In October 2000, Toronto came calling again. This time it was a television host position. The show was called *imagineNATIVE*, and it aired on the Aboriginal Peoples Television Network (APTN). With her easy manner, attractive magnetism, and great fashion sense, Nicole slipped into this role effortlessly. (The show *imagineNATIVE* was such a success that it evolved into an international media arts festival in 2001, showcasing Aboriginal films, videos, and hands-on workshops.)

Nicole honed her communication skills further, working at the National Aboriginal Achievement Foundation for six months before landing a steady position back at APTN in April 2001. Nicole adored her job as a video journalist. When the news anchor was on holiday, Nicole was invited to take this role. These were exciting times for 27-year-old Nicole.

Still, something was amiss. Toronto's skyscrapers, hustle and bustle, and congestion weren't to Nicole's liking. The corporate lifestyle disagreed with her spiritual values. She told her supervisor she was resigning and moving back to the West. In an effort to keep their valued team member, the station offered Nicole exciting work in Alberta. She agreed and opened the first Prairie bureau for APTN in Edmonton. Nicole busily traveled around Alberta and Saskatchewan, filing news stories related to Aboriginal issues. There was no shortage of stories to chase down, and she was doing exactly what she had dreamed of – or was she?

Nicole wrote news stories about Aboriginal peoples, but she found the topics very negative. Nicole said, "I was at a place where this was getting tiresome. It was sort of bringing my spirits down." Nicole continued, "I was thinking to myself: *What can I be doing that's not going to be so entrenched in some of these extreme, gut-wrenching stories and negative feelings?*

Nicole Robertson where she likes to be –
behind the camera, shooting a video.

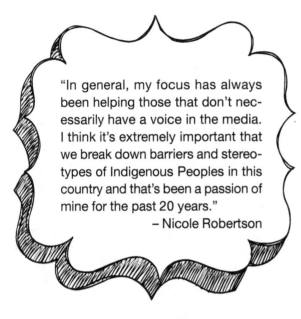

"In general, my focus has always been helping those that don't necessarily have a voice in the media. I think it's extremely important that we break down barriers and stereotypes of Indigenous Peoples in this country and that's been a passion of mine for the past 20 years."
– Nicole Robertson

"All this thinking led to this serious and daunting question: *How can I break into this area of owning my own business?*

"The following day," Nicole explained, "I was on my way to the news station, and I was at this intersection, and this truck came out of nowhere and took off. It was a hit and run. It was a five-car pile-up. I had extreme whiplash. I had to go through physiotherapy. I had two or three months to decide how to proceed with my business. And through that time out, and [being] alone, I came up with Muskwa Productions."

In May 2002, Nicole launched her business. "I went out and got some information through the registry office, registered my business, and came up with a name. You know all the things: logo, design, and colors. [It was a] very creative time. I enjoyed that, actually. It was the beginning of something fresh and new."

A year after launching her own business, Nicole had the opportunity to work for the Assembly of First Nations in Alberta. She did this for two years, balancing her work-related tasks with her most exciting venture ever – becoming a mom in 2004, at age 30. She named her daughter *Sequan* [see-kwan], which means "spring" in Cree. Nicole said, like spring, her daughter embodies "growth, change, beauty, freshness."

Names are important to Nicole, who was deeply honored to receive her own Native name from a Blackfoot elder in the summer of 2010. *Api'siipistaaki* [ahh-pee-see-pis-too-ah-kee] means "White Owl Woman." An owl represents a messenger, which suits the way she continuously brings good news to people through the media, and also harkens back to her

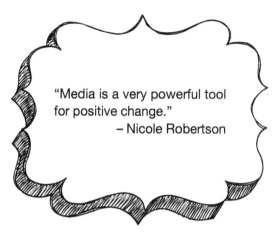

"Media is a very powerful tool for positive change."
– Nicole Robertson

grandfather. White, is a symbol of purity – perfect for the good, positive news that resonates best with Nicole.

At Muskwa Productions, Nicole works hard to bring good-news stories about Aboriginal peoples to the general public. "I'm always looking at ways to get our perspective included in stories that are being told locally, regionally, and nationally through the news media." She produces educational and informative videos for many different associations, including the United Way's Aboriginal Pride Program. Nicole has applied her savvy marketing strategies to the Aboriginal Health Program for the Alberta Cancer Board. Her name is found at the bottom of countless well-researched, informative press releases. Nicole sends these news briefs to major newspapers, radio stations, and TV stations, on topics related to Aboriginal treaty issues, new government policies, and health and employment initiatives, to name a few. These actions help get the word out so that Canadians can be properly informed about Aboriginal issues and current events. "I like to think of myself as a spin doctor as I plug our stories in the media," Nicole explained.

Nicole is quick to lend her services to generous individuals who are trying to change the world by helping Indigenous People in need. For example, Nicole stepped in and wrote a press release to assist a Cree man who wanted to encourage his community members to donate items for the Attawapiskat First Nation in northern Ontario. (That nation was in the midst of a housing crisis in the winter of 2011, and families were lacking basic necessities.) With her extensive media connections, the man's message spread far and wide, helping him achieve his goal. Clearly, Nicole is a kind and generous entrepreneur who continually seeks out opportunities with others to bring about change. "I'm blessed that I can have a career [that] doesn't feel like work. I'm passionate about what I do and that's why I do everything to the best of my abilities."

Now that Muskwa Productions is a thriving business, Nicole is thrilled to be able to give her daughter opportunities that she didn't have as a child. Mother and daughter live on the Tsuu T'Ina [soot-tenna] Nation, just southwest of Calgary, in a sustainable community where people are "not allowed to put up fences or cut down trees." Nicole loves her neighborhood. "You go outside and there are 20-foot pine trees and a big blue sky, and the foothills of the Rocky Mountains, and a river streaming close by. And you just know that there's a grander thing to life and the Creator is at the center of it all."

Nicole Robertson knows who she is – a woman who is proud of her roots and committed to making a difference to society. She takes great pleasure in sharing her knowledge about Aboriginal culture and spreading good news – and, the news just keeps getting better. Without a doubt, this accomplished and caring entrepreneur is a gifted messenger who is living her dream.

From Flag Girl to CEO with Attitude
Kelsey Ramsden

1976 -

Ayoung girl puts the last strokes of vibrant crayon on her drawing and then skips over to the pre-school teacher. She beams with pride. The teacher, "Auntie Flo," looks into Kelsey's sparkling green eyes and says, "That's a really good picture, but you've got it wrong!"

Kelsey is bewildered. She loves her artwork. *What's wrong with it?* she wonders, looking down at the two yellow suns.

"There's only *one* sunshine," Auntie Flo explains.

I know there's really only one sunshine, thinks five-year-old Kelsey, quietly fuming. *But this picture has two! This is just what it is.*

Years later, Kelsey often recalled this vivid memory, which

marked a defining moment for her. It made her realize that other people could misunderstand her ideas, skewing them into something distorted and wrong. Now grown up, Kelsey says, "Find something you're legitimately passionate about.... If you believe in it, try it." She adds, "I don't pay attention to what other people are saying. They often think I'm crazy. That's OK. It doesn't matter." Indeed, if everyone is doing something one way, Kelsey is much more apt to try it her own special way. In a school of fish following the current, this gal is the one swimming the other way. And uncharted waters don't scare her one bit.

Kelsey Kitsch lived in a beautiful lakefront home in Kelowna, British Columbia, for most of her childhood. During the hot, sunny summers, Kelsey and her younger brother, Trent, used to swim in Okanagan Lake and play in the forest, building forts, throwing rocks, and exploring. Winter pastimes included sledding, skiing, and building snow forts. At age 12, Kelsey's family moved down the street, and then to a different – but still very nice – neighborhood, when she was 14. They moved again when she was 16, staying within the same area. No matter where she lived, Kelsey's house was always full of friends and family – and lots of kids. Kelsey remembers, "If we didn't have a lake, we had a pool. We always had water."

As budding entrepreneurs, Kelsey and Trent were constantly coming up with money-making schemes. "We'd sell juice, or make cupcakes, or put on shows," she recalled. Sometimes the pair would sweep a large portion of the street they lived on and try to charge their neighbors money to drive past. Standard jobs, like babysitting and delivering newspapers, didn't interest Kelsey very much. She preferred to come up with her own ideas. At her three different elementary schools, Kelsey's favorite classes were math and art. She sure seemed to have a knack for creativity.

From grade 8 to 12, Kelsey attended Kelowna Secondary

School. She still liked math – even though her marks weren't very good – and also playing tenor saxophone in the band, cooking, and woodworking. Her favorite thing about school, however, was socializing with friends and playing sports. Back in elementary school, she played soccer and then switched to competitive swimming. In grade 4, she started to play softball and in grade 6 added basketball. She continued with these two sports through to grade 12. During her high school years, she also played field hockey and rugby. The team coach chose Kelsey to be team captain, year after year. Even in sports in which she didn't excel so much – like basketball – Kelsey was appointed team captain.

"I would say sports were a huge part of [my] developing leadership skills," she admits. In this role she learned how to be both a team member and the boss. She always included all the players and didn't give the "jocks" more attention than the "artsy" girls. If they were members of the team, Kelsey made sure they were treated with respect. She also learned how to keep her strong feelings and passions at bay and to not verbally lambast other players for slipping up during a game: "That person is not going to work

Kelsey's lively confidence and individuality are clear in this school photo from grade 6.

harder for my team if I call them out in front of everyone else," she explained.

After finishing grade 9, Kelsey landed her first paid job. She worked for her dad's construction company, way up north on the Alaska Highway in the Yukon, close to the border of British Columbia. She was going to be a flag person – the roadside worker who holds up the "Slow" or "Stop" sign to direct traffic during road construction. There, surrounded by fir trees and lakes, "in the middle of nowhere," 14-year-old

Entrepreneurial Women in Construction

Julissa Carielo, president, Tejas Premier Building Contractor Inc., San Antonio, Texas
- "I loved the industry from the start."

Sandy Hussey, retired welder, Seattle, Washington
- "No matter what you do, just go out and do your best job."

Deanna Johnson, Nations Construction & Consulting, Chilliwack, British Columbia
- "… there was a real need for quality homes for First Nations people…There are challenges, especially when you first start out, because a lot of people just don't think that women can do construction."

Chelsea Orvis, heavy equipment operator, Fort McMurray, Alberta
- "I enjoy what I'm doing."

Ruth Wilford, owner/operator at Renovations Ruth, Toronto, Ontario
- "I enjoy working with designers, engineers, and architects. I like to bring out the best in everyone, and get the job done quickly, safely, and efficiently. I love sourcing out products and new green technology. Making someone's dream come true is the best feeling!"

Kelsey joined on as the youngest member of a work crew entirely made up of men, all at least ten years older than her. The only other female was the camp cook. When Don Tasker, the foreman, found out who Kelsey's dad, Bruce, had hired, his first response was, "I am not a babysitter!" But Bruce was the boss, and the job was Kelsey's – as long as she worked hard.

About two weeks after arriving, Kelsey turned 15. What a way to spend a birthday!

Kelsey's Tips for Young Entrepreneurs

- Be positive!
- Find something you are passionate about
- Don't get hung up on what other people say, especially if it's critical feedback
- Seek out mentors in the industry you're interested in. Ask them questions
- Make a to-do list every night before you go to bed, outlining your tasks for the next day
- Be prepared to "pivot" – change according to challenges
- Work hard – really hard!

Surrounded by black flies, standing on the highway, waiting for vehicles to approach, Kelsey was bored. Worse, she knew her friends in Kelowna were having heaps of fun. Cooped up in a tiny room – barely bigger than her single bed – in a rugged worksite trailer, Kelsey spent lots of nights crying herself to sleep. She hated her job.

One morning, Kelsey showed up late for work. Don's reply was harsh: "Look, you're working for free today, kid. You think your time is better than mine?" Then he gave her the worst jobs all day long. Rather than getting upset or calling home or quitting, Kelsey thought, *You're either going to cave or gristle up. OK! Let's go then.* She was never late for work again – ever. Indeed, she admits, "It taught me a lot of lessons. And then, after I was there for a while, [I] just got into the groove of

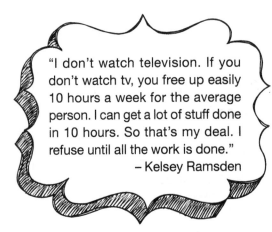

"I don't watch television. If you don't watch tv, you free up easily 10 hours a week for the average person. I can get a lot of stuff done in 10 hours. So that's my deal. I refuse until all the work is done."
– Kelsey Ramsden

being out there and working hard. Then I started to like it." Kelsey sums up her satisfaction with the job this way: "I liked the people I worked with, and I liked the product. At the end of the day, seeing that...we built that!" Her pride in being part of the construction team is solid – just like the road she helped build. To this day, Kelsey respects Don for not treating her differently because she was the boss's kid and a girl.

Kelsey continued working for her dad on road-construction sites during the summer holidays. Her dad's strong work ethic rubbed off. After school, Kelsey took on a variety of part-time jobs. For a while she delivered papers for a law office. She had a number of coffee-shop jobs, which were fun because she could hang out and talk to friends. Even then, Kelsey knew she was willing to work hard, but she didn't like working for other people. For her, these jobs felt like she was just "clocking in, clocking out." But Kelsey wanted to be free. She was determined to do what she loved and was willing to take risks to make it happen. In short, she already possessed some of the key characteristics of a successful entrepreneur.

Kelsey spent some of her money on trendy T-shirts and candy, but there are limits to how much a person can spend on items like that. Her dad asked her and Trent, who'd also been working a lot, what they were going to do with their money. Kelsey's first thought was to buy a car. She was 18, and having her own car was appealing. Her dad said, "No you're not. That's ridiculous!" Instead, he laid out a few options. One idea was to invest in a ski-hill property with a group of trusted adults.

Kelsey and Trent decided to go for it. Their family lawyer created a company for the two of them from a list of company names he had already incorporated. They chose Belevedere Place Development from the list of pre-named and numbered companies. (They didn't have any say in the actual name.) Then, with the other partners, they created a second company that actually bought the land. This was Kelsey's first investment. She was getting a taste of entrepreneurship at a very young age.

After graduating from high school in 1994, Kelsey enrolled at Okanagan University College (now Okanagan College) in Kelowna for a year. Next, she moved to Victoria, B.C., and went to Camosun College. Kelsey recalls that while she was there one of her roommates said something like, "Oh, it doesn't matter. Kelsey doesn't have to study. She doesn't care about her marks anyway." Kelsey says, "It really hit me, like – wait a minute – these people are defining me, and my intelligence, by my grades?" Not only was Kelsey offended by this comment, she was also stirred into action. After that, she hit the books and studied diligently. Before long she had straight A's and won acceptance to the University of Victoria. She graduated in 1999 with a BA in economics. From there, she spent two-and-a-half years working for construction companies. Then, prompted by her father – a Masters of Business Administration (MBA) graduate – she applied to 12 different MBA programs and was accepted at the Richard Ivey School of Business at Western University in London, Ontario. Later on, she found out how she'd managed to scrape in. Her application lay forgotten in the "do not admit" pile, until an administrator noticed it for its unique, colorful, and different approach and persuaded others to put her at the top of the waiting list. An accepted student declined and Kelsey was in, with only two weeks' notice. At Ivey, Kelsey honed her business-related thinking, or thought processes, and learned the value of remaining calm during a crisis.

Rub Shoulders with Other Women in the Construction Biz

These organizations can offer support to women pursuing a career (or a business) in construction:

Association of Women Contractors (AWC), St. Paul, Minnesota
• Provides educational and professional resources to female business owners in the construction industry

Canadian Association of Women in Construction (CAWIC), Mississauga, Ontario
• Non-profit organization that supports the success of women in construction-related fields

Canadian Construction Women (CCW), Vancouver, British Columbia
• Networking and mentoring opportunities for women working in construction

National Association of Women in Construction (NAWIC), Fort Worth, Texas
• Support network for women working in construction

Women Building Futures (WBF), Edmonton, Alberta
• Non-profit organization that trains women in construction-related occupations, such as welder, electrician, pipe fitter, or heavy equipment operator; includes housing for single women

Women Construction Owners & Executives (WCOE), Alexandria, Virginia
• Organization that brings together and supports women entrepreneurs in construction

Women in Construction (WINC), Toronto, Ontario
• Non-profit organization that helps individuals in need

Kelsey met her husband-to-be, fellow student Andrew Ramsden, at a pre-accounting study group at Ivey. The two were wed a year after graduating, in 2005. They spent six months working as consultants in Toronto, but Kelsey was miserable with the slow pace at which her recommendations were implemented – if ever – and she realized, "This is totally not me. I want to start a construction company. The best place for me to do that is in B.C." The couple devised a long-term plan. They agreed to move to Kelowna for five years and then back to London, so that Andrew could fulfill his dream of buying out a family business from his uncle.

In 2005, Kelsey re-launched Belvedere Place Development as a construction company in Kelowna. She designed the company to serve any and all needs that involve moving earth. This would include building roads, highways, runways, bridges, or installing storm sewers and pipes. (Kelsey's brother was no longer involved in Belvedere Place Development after 2005.) She got to work hiring a top-notch crew of trustworthy, skilled workers, and made sure they all got along.

One of her biggest pet peeves when she started was when employees pointed out what was wrong without suggesting solutions. Kelsey would think to herself: "I can see that. I didn't hire you to tell me what I already know. I hired you to come up with a solution." After all, in her mind, problems were "always happening," but solving problems was where creativity and ingenuity could emerge. What's more, coming up with excellent solutions would ultimately lead to success – lots of success.

In the beginning, Kelsey aimed for government contracts. This worked out very well for her. However, when the recession hit in 2009, winning contracts became much tougher, and profits plummeted. Many companies went out of business, and Kelsey didn't want to join them. Instead, her instinct was to "reinvent," and that's exactly what she did. She expanded

Kelsey shares a laugh with a worker on a job site at Ootsa Lake
in northern British Columbia. Her company used a special material
called roller-compacted concrete to build a dam.

into working for private companies and developed sound relationships with businesspeople, based on trust, honesty, and integrity. Kelsey communicated clearly with her clients, other business partners, and on-site foremen with regular updates by phone and email. Frequent communication kept her clients on side, trusting her and her team. Honesty was, and is, always the best policy.

Andrew moved to London as planned in 2010, taking their three-year-old daughter, Sophie, with him. Kelsey remained in B.C. for another six or seven months, working on a job on the Alaska Highway. Living apart from her daughter during that time was a huge sacrifice, but Kelsey saw this as a necessary part of being a CEO. Her son Graeme was born in 2010. Without missing a beat, Kelsey was back to work with her infant son "on her hip." (It had been no different after Sophie's birth.) Kelsey resumed commuting back and forth between London and Kelowna. Then, when a second son, Sam, arrived in 2011, Kelsey put management in place at her British Columbia-based company and put a stop to the frequent traveling. Now, mother to three children under five, Kelsey made a choice to spend more time at home.

Abruptly, on January 13, 2012, Kelsey faced her greatest challenge ever. She was diagnosed with cancer. It was a rare type that spreads quickly. Two weeks later, Kelsey had an operation. Then, in April, she had a second, more extensive surgery. She was very lucky that the cancerous cells were found early and were removed completely. Kelsey can breathe easier now because she beat the odds. She counts her blessings every day. During the two-month recovery period, the women in her family – her extraordinary mom and her generous aunts – pulled together and helped out. Relying on family helped Kelsey get through the difficult time.

By July, Kelsey – now 36 – was keen to get back into

action. After an extended family holiday out West, she got to work launching a new company called SparkPlay. The company's focus is on encouraging children and parents to play together, turn off electronic devices, and be creative. It's a world apart from road construction.

By 2012, Belvedere Place Development employed eight full-time and 58 part-time staff. Kelsey had built a multi-million-dollar company, despite the challenges. Then came public recognition. *Chatelaine* and *PROFIT* magazines honored Kelsey Ramsden as Canada's number-one woman entrepreneur. This led to more media attention and requests to be in the spotlight. Even so, industrious Kelsey is much more likely to be found researching another new business venture than boasting about her past successes. These days, she fills her spare time mentoring young entrepreneurs or giving guest lectures at the Ivey School of Business. After all, she has a long to-do list, and hardworking Kelsey's on a mission to get the job done – very, very well.

Making Clean Water Her Business
Jodi Glover

1979 -

R ain drops begin to spatter and form little rivers on the windshield. Jodi flicks on the wipers and sweeps her bangs across her forehead, tucking a loose strand behind her ear. The saying "Put your best foot forward" runs through her head. This is something her mother used to say to her every day before school.

During her less-than-20-minute commute to work in the morning, she is running late. She didn't fill her travel mug before getting out the door, and today she's actually forgotten it completely. Jodi knows she could easily pull off the highway and stop at a coffee shop, but the recycling program in her region doesn't accept paper coffee cups. Disposable cups must go in the garbage. Jodi always considers people and the planet, and this morning, she opts to forgo her hot beverage. Her concern for the environment runs deep.

The young business owner smiles and laughs at a joyful burst of song from her toddler in the back seat. Her kids are a great reminder of what is really important. Missing out on a coffee isn't a big deal. In a couple of minutes, she'll drop off Tyler at his daycare, which is just around the corner from her company. Jodi wonders how her six-year-old son's day is going. She's a proud mom who takes great delight in her two children.

Watching rainwater splash on the surface of the highway, Jodi's thoughts shift to water – along with her family, it's her greatest passion. She thinks back to a life-changing experience she had in Central America when she was 20. As part of an expedition, organized by her local church, Jodi spent hot, sunny days playing with children outside an orphan-

age. The experience changed the way she saw the world – and water. She learned that people cannot take water for granted and that clean drinking water is vital for our health. Jodi thinks about this every time she turns on a tap and every time she arrives at work – enthusiastic and highly motivated.

Jodi Hallett was born in Scarborough, Ontario, but moved to nearby Pickering when she was really young. She grew up in a house on a dead-end street with her mom, Brenda, her dad, Ron,

Even as a young child, Jodi loved being near the water.

and her older brother, Matthew. Jodi remembers "tons of kids" playing outside in her neighborhood. Kick-the-can and hide-and-go seek were fun ways to pass the time. But young Jodi was never idle. At age five, she sold lemonade with her best friend. She remembers "being so proud as we sat there waiting for someone to purchase our lemonade."

By age ten, Jodi had launched her own jewelry business, making bracelets from plastic laces called gimp. Her father – who was a mechanical engineer and later launched his own business – was very supportive of this venture. "He actually lent me money so I could buy big rolls of gimp." This helped Jodi keep her costs down. Her dad taught her that buying materials in bulk would be much cheaper than purchasing individual strands. To make her business as real as possible, Jodi designed her own letterhead with a little butterfly logo. Next, Jodi hired a friend to be her secretary. She asked her friend to call everyone in her parents' phone book to see if they wanted to buy some handmade jewelry. Jodi also sold her bracelets and earrings at garage sales.

At age 11, the young entrepreneur began delivering news-papers once a week, after school. She kept this up through rain, shine, and snowstorms until she was 15, earning about $11 a month. When she turned 12, Jodi was keen to take a babysitting course and start looking after kids. Whenever she was hired, she'd arrive with a large tub filled with books, toys, and craft supplies. She'd take the children to the park and then encourage them to write a story, make puppets, and put on a show. When Jodi was 14 or 15, she babysat all day long for the whole summer. She earned about $10 a day while her friends were having fun playing video games or just hanging out together. Even with this money coming in, Jodi continued to look for ways to earn more. She recalls, "I saved everything."

Throughout her childhood and teenage years, Jodi par-ticipated enthusiastically in a wide range of activities. She took lessons in piano, jazz, ballet, and tap, as well as trampoline, swimming, and drama. She played soccer and volleyball. During high school, she joined the skiing club and the field hockey team. Jodi was competitive by nature, and her love of sports and her fearlessness led to many injuries. She broke her leg just before her sixth birthday in a tobogganing accident. Next, she fractured her thumb playing volleyball at school. After that, 12-year-old Jodi was carried off the court and transported by ambulance when she broke her nose during a dodge ball game at sports camp. The injury-prone athlete broke her thumb a second time while playing field hockey at high school. After one such incident, Jodi earned the award for "the athlete

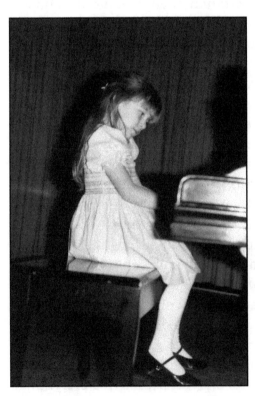

who takes a licking and keeps on ticking." Years later, this never-stay-down attitude would be an advantage when Jodi became an entrepreneur.

Jodi found English classes difficult in high school, but she always tried her best. Overall, she achieved very good marks and earned a spot on the Honor Roll. When she wasn't hanging out with her close group of friends, attending practices or trying to beat her classmates in timed math quizzes, Jodi kept busy juggling jobs. "I worked a lot," she remembers.

Jodi wasn't one to sit still, unless of course, she was playing the piano.

"I always had a part-time job." No doubt scheduling homework, teams, clubs, and work meant she developed smart time-management skills.

Math was Jodi's strongest subject, and so she set her sights on a career in accounting. After graduating from Dunbarton High School in Pickering, Jodi pushed hard to save up more money with "three part-time jobs in the summer leading up to university." Then, in September 1998, she moved to Hamilton, Ontario, and chose as many accounting and math courses as she could fit into her timetable. As usual, math came easily to her. "I remember getting over 100 percent on my Calculus exam," Jodi admits, explaining that the professor had to adjust the class's marks to reduce the high number of failing grades, pushing Jodi's mark over 100. Jodi kept quiet about her impressive grades – which included 98 percent in accounting and high 90s in other math and science courses – thinking it wasn't cool to be smart.

Working Holiday

After her first year at university, Jodi spent one week in Guatemala as a volunteer. She helped distribute food, build a house, and assist at an orphanage. Then, back at university, she was inspired to take some peace studies courses. Jodi's experience in a developing country, coupled with her studies, deeply affected her: "It opened my understanding to the world in which we live, and it still keeps me grounded and appreciative today." She adds, "That's never really left me."

In her first year at McMaster University, Jodi became friends with Andrew Glover, a software engineering student. After a couple of years, they became girlfriend and boyfriend. Also at McMaster, Jodi met Dan Shaver, a fellow commerce student, whom she would later hire to work for her company.

Then, in the summer of 2001, just before starting her

"My mom always said I liked a challenge when I was a kid, and I think that still holds true."
– Jodi Glover

fourth year, Jodi took part in a government program designed to assist young entrepreneurs. She wanted her business to promote environment-friendly practices, and so she created a solar heating company. Jodi received a small start-up grant to help offset business expenses and attended weekly meetings with an experienced business professional who acted as her mentor. To this day, Jodi describes this as "an amazing opportunity" and says it showed her that "textbooks can only teach you so much." She remembers working really hard, learning lots, but not making any money. An end-of-program subsidy helped make up for the loss she incurred. Jodi credits this summer job as being hugely influential. It helped her understand the importance of profitability to a healthy, successful business. Next time – and surely there'd be a next time – she'd keep a closer watch on profit margins.

After running her own small business, the idea of being a chartered accountant no longer inspired Jodi. Instead, she wanted to be an entrepreneur and was determined to do "something good for the environment." Abruptly, Jodi changed her plan. "I dropped every accounting course and took entrepreneurship, sales, and marketing for my last year." Jodi graduated in 2002, earning an Honors Bachelor of Commerce degree.

At 23, the new graduate eagerly joined Scotiabank in Scarborough, Ontario, as a small business adviser. She worked there for a year, gaining more valuable experience.

"It was really, really good exposure to have that [experience] and see all the different kinds of companies that are out there, and what they go through and the struggles." Helping small business owners secure financing underlined the importance of sound

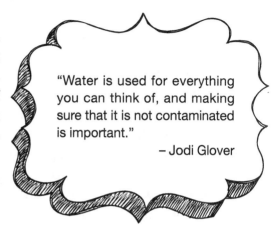

"Water is used for everything you can think of, and making sure that it is not contaminated is important."

– Jodi Glover

finances in growing a business. Yet her customers noticed that Jodi seemed to be on the wrong side of the desk. "Why aren't you one of us?" they'd say, temptingly.

In August 2003, Jodi Hallett married Andrew Glover. On their honeymoon, Jodi recalls saying to her husband, "One day it would be so nice to have a business together." The newlyweds talked about her dream of having a green tech company and making a difference in the world. When they returned home to Markham, Ontario, Andrew – who was skilled at making things – started tinkering in his spare time.

When Jodi left her job at Scotiabank, she went to work for her father at a Toronto-based company called UV Pure Technologies, which he had founded when she was in high school. (Jodi had grown up learning about treating water from her dad who used to work for a large company that made UV – ultraviolet – disinfection systems.) At UV Pure, Jodi expanded her knowledge of cleaning water with ultraviolet rays. This environment-friendly process uses fewer chemicals like chlorine, which are often added to water to make it safe to drink. Instead, UV purification relies on ultraviolet light to purify water. This method is a little more expensive than adding chemicals, but it is kinder to the Earth – and healthier, too. By working in sales and marketing at her dad's company for about a year, Jodi gained a firm foundation in this industry.

Meanwhile, Andrew's tinkering was taking shape. One day he said to Jodi, "I've got an idea and I want to try it out." He explained that he thought he could invent a small, portable device that would analyze water for contaminants. The instrument – like no other – would provide instant, accurate results. To create a prototype, he'd need to buy about $200 worth of parts. Money was tight, but Jodi was all for it. She thought the concept was clever and appealing. Jodi explained, "Then I started working on figuring out how I could take his idea and turn it into an actual business. I looked at the market, and there was definitely a need for it!"

Andrew continued working at his engineering job, but Jodi left UV Pure and started building a new business, selling Andrew's device. Andrew applied for a patent for his device, and Jodi got to work. First, she registered her company, which she called Real Tech, Inc. Then, she sourced parts, created a budget, looked for customers, and explored sales and marketing opportunities. When a first order came in for 20 units, Jodi was ecstatic. She scraped together enough money to buy the parts to fulfill this order. More money was required, however, and more orders were bound to come in. Jodi lamented, "If we just had a little bit more money then we could do *this* marketing effort, and we could go to *that* trade show, and we could tell the world that we exist just a little bit more. That would help grow the sales." Raising the price of their device was not an option for Jodi.

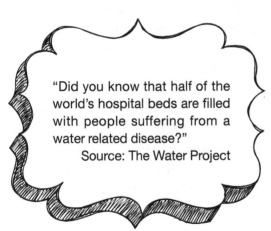

"Did you know that half of the world's hospital beds are filled with people suffering from a water related disease?"
Source: The Water Project

She wanted to keep the costs down, making their instrument accessible to water treatment plants in local communities and worldwide. As Jodi passionately describes it, "I go to bed at night and – literally since I started the company – I think, if I could get these units all over the world – everywhere – we'd save lives! I mean, people won't be drinking contaminated water." She adds, "Improving water quality is our universal goal."

Jodi bought a large world map and hung it on the wall in her home office. She placed one red dot on the map at the location of the company that placed the first order. Then she vowed,

Zach, Andrew, Jodi, and Tyler enjoy some memorable holiday time together in their home. Family and water are Jodi's two passions.

Excellent Eco-Entrepreneurs

This new field offers a huge scope for entrepreneurs. From creating new products out of discarded or recycled materials to improving packaging and alternative sources of energy, these eco-entrepreneurs are changing the world in a beautiful way. Go green!

Susanna Carson, founder and CEO of BSI Biodegradable Solutions, Vancouver, British Columbia
• Designs and creates compostable packaging and products for the food-service industry

Reese Fernandez-Ruiz, co-founder of Rags2Riches Inc., Manila, the Philippines
• Partners with local fashion designers to provide industrious women with fair wages and access to scraps of discarded cloth to create rugs, purses, and handbags; helps women escape poverty

Eden Full, founder of Roseicollis Technologies Inc., Calgary, Alberta, and San Francisco, California
• Manufactures a device that makes solar energy cheaper and more accessible

Krystal O'Mara, founder of ReMain Eco Design and Consulting, Amarillo, Texas
• Designs, builds, and sells furniture made from recycled bicycle parts – including a chandelier made from old bike wheels and rims

"One day there's going to be red dots all over." Before long, she made a sale in the United States, then one in Australia. More and more red dots appeared on her map. Seeing her company's reach expanding internationally was exciting.

Andrew cut back his engineering job to part-time so he could focus more intently on Real Tech with Jodi. In January 2006, he left his job, but continued doing some consulting work on the side. Many friends thought the Glovers were crazy, and Jodi is quick to admit it was a struggle: "We never watched TV. We didn't go out. We didn't take a vacation or anything." With the growth they were achieving, however, they were able to lease a small office space. Now Jodi didn't have to convince clients to meet her in coffee shops or make believe that Real Tech had a professional office and a staff. In fact, the company now had three employees (Jodi, Andrew, and Jodi's cousin, Jay) and four walls! With its growing list of clients, the business was gaining credibility – and that was very good for sales.

Shortly after they moved in to the new office space, Jodi found out she was pregnant. She worked throughout her pregnancy, seeking new clients and demonstrating the UV device until she had to go to the hospital. She asked if she could take a laptop and continue working, but the hospital staff denied her request. As Jodi and Andrew welcomed their son, Zachary, into the world, clients wondered why Jodi hadn't responded to their messages over those few days. (In contrast, most moms – and some dads – disappear for weeks after the arrival of a new baby.) "It was just a crazy time. We were busy, and growing a business, and having a baby," Jodi remembers, with a smile. After an absence of three business days, plus a weekend, Jodi returned to work with baby Zach snuggled in her arms. When Zach slept, Jodi worked. Newborns sleep a lot, so this arrangement was effective. As time went by, however,

The UN declared 2013 the International Year of Water Cooperation, highlighting the importance of water around the world.

Jodi and Andrew learned that their son had asthma and some severe food allergies. This meant Zach wouldn't be able to attend daycare as expected. He required one-on-one attention to ensure he was kept safe.

Jodi's mom, Brenda, offered to care for Zach three days a week. Jodi and Andrew were very grateful. What's more, by that time Brenda was on staff at Real Tech, taking care of accounting – so she was busy. Over the next few years, amidst all this juggling, the company continued to grow, slowly but surely. In hiring new staff, Jodi sought hardworking professionals who got along with the other team players, liked responsibility, and embraced challenges. In 2009, Jodi hired her university friend Dan to assist with sales and later Wanda Janes to handle the bookkeeping. The business was now six-employees strong, and the phone just kept ringing. Then, Jodi's dad came on board, after selling UV Pure. Real Tech was a tight-knit family, in more ways than one!

In April 2010, Jodi leased a new office that was twice the size of the old one. She also hired five new employees. Life got busier still when a second son, Tyler, arrived in the fall. Then, Jodi had their office renovated in the summer of 2011, nearly doubling its size again. Along with offices, work stations, a boardroom, a kitchen, and a large, open-concept manufacturing area, the renovation plan included a playroom for the staff's children. Zach and Tyler use this area most, but employees sometimes bring in children, too. Jodi commends her 15 devoted and hard-working staff members saying, "We're more like a team of 30."

With someone as successful as Jodi, it stands to reason that she has been publically recognized numerous times. Environmentalist David Suzuki presented Jodi with the Deloitte Technology Green 15™ Award every year from 2009 to 2012. The award recognizes companies that conserve energy and use resources wisely. In 2012, Jodi received an RBC Canadian Women Entrepreneur Award for the category "Sustainability." She was honored as one of six award winners from a pool of 3,500 women. Most recently, *Water Canada* magazine recognized Jodi as a key figure in Canada's water industry. She is featured in the Water's Next 2013 publication for being one of "Canada's Best and Brightest in Water."

Jodi describes her own role as "constantly evolving." These days, she spends more time making big decisions, planning strategically for future growth, and taking care of high-level administrative challenges. She looks forward to energetic meetings with her dynamic sales team. In the winter months, Jodi jokes with her staff, "Everyone bring your snow pants tomorrow. We need to do a walk and talk – it's been a while!" Reconnecting with staff, chatting, and brainstorming while also getting some fresh air and exercise and is a winning combination for Jodi, who is a people person a multi-tasking pro.

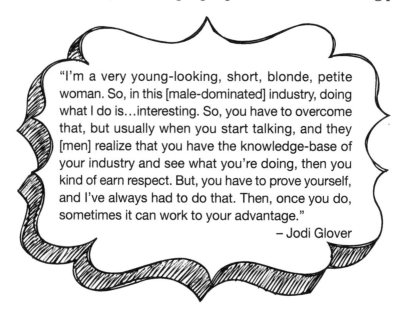

"I'm a very young-looking, short, blonde, petite woman. So, in this [male-dominated] industry, doing what I do is…interesting. So, you have to overcome that, but usually when you start talking, and they [men] realize that you have the knowledge-base of your industry and see what you're doing, then you kind of earn respect. But, you have to prove yourself, and I've always had to do that. Then, once you do, sometimes it can work to your advantage."

– Jodi Glover

Jodi makes time for groups of children who visit Real Tech to learn about clean water. She also donates time to her community by sitting on the Water Quality Advisory Board at Durham College. She brings a vibrant industry perspective to these meetings.

Jodi's map of the world from her first year in business still serves as an inspirational tool. At last count, red dots cover 37 different countries. What an accomplishment in eight years! Jodi continues to "raise the bar" and set more goals for herself and her company. In her characteristic rapid-fire delivery, she states passionately, "I still have so much more I want to achieve." That's good news for people who understand the importance of clean, safe drinking water.

Glossary

Alumni: Graduates from a university, college, or school

BA: A Bachelor of Arts degree; a three- or four-year university program

Board of Directors: A group made up of some, or all, of a company's executive-level businesspeople and also outside, expert advisers who are elected or chosen to oversee the operations of a company; a business's key decision-makers who set policies and goals and are responsible for the company's actions

CEO: A chief executive officer; the head of a company; a high-ranking business executive

Client: A customer; someone who buys products or services

COO: A chief operations officer or director of operations; often second in command after the CEO; a high-ranking business executive

Customer loyalty: The devotion of satisfied shoppers toward a company, its products and services; the strong support of people who willingly purchase a company's products or services again and again

Direct marketing: Selling products and services straight to the customer through home parties, personal emails, text messages, or phone calls; sales efforts that target a specific group of people, such as homeowners

Eco-entrepreneur: An entrepreneur who bases her company on principles of conserving resources and protecting the planet, for example, a manufacturer of eco-friendly packaging; a business leader who measures the environmental impact of her company, along with profits, when assessing her company's succcess.

Executive: A high-ranking business-person in a company

Investor: Someone who agrees to lend money to a company in hopes that she will receive profits over time; shareholder

Market: A group of customers who may be interested in purchasing a product or service

MBA: A Masters of Business Administration degree; a one- or two-year graduate-level university program geared toward students who wish to become successful in business as owners, executives, or managers

Negotiate: The act of two or more people, associations, or

groups trying to come to an agreement even when they have conflicting interests or ideas.

Product: Something that is for sale, for example, T-shirts or lemonade

Promotion: A special event or offer that encourages customers to buy a certain product or service; an activity that is meant to increase the demand for a product or service; a change of job title within a company, usually bringing with it increased responsibility and salary

Service: Useful labor that people need or want, for example, babysitting, car washing, and dog walking

Shareholder: Someone who invests money in a company that is owned by many members of the public; one of many lenders who hopes to earn a profit over time

Social Entrepreneur: An entrepreneur who bases her company on principles of social responsibility; a business leader who measures the impact on society of her company, along with profits, when assessing her company's success, for example, a water company that uses its profits to bring safe, clean drinking water to people in developing countries

Start-up Money: A lump sum of money that helps the founder launch a new company and pay for expenses, such as rent, salaries, and office equipment

Sources

Madam C.J. Walker

Black Beauty: Millionaire C.J. Walker
http://www.scholastic.com/teachers/article/
black-beauty-millionaire-c-j-walker

Bundles, A'Lelia. *On Her Own Ground: The Life and Times of Madam C.J. Walker.* New York, NY: Washington Square Press, 2001.

DOL Celebrates Women's History Month (A'Lelia Bundles)
http://www.youtube.com/watch?v=q4lbpm_LQSU

The Great Leaders Series: Madam C.J. Walker, Founder of Madam C.J. Walker Enterprises
http://www.inc.com/30years/articles/madam-cj-walker.html

Krohn, Katherine. *Madam C.J. Walker: Pioneer Businesswoman.* Mankato, MN: Capstone Press, 2008.

Madam C.J. Walker
http://www.madamewalker.net/
http://www.gardenofpraise.com/ibdwalker.htm

http://en.wikipedia.org/wiki/Madam_C._J._Walker
http://www.gale.cengage.com/free_resources/bhm/bio/walker_s.htm
http://www.mygrowthplan.org/Biographies/MadamC.J.Walker.htm

Madam C.J. Walker Biography
http://www.biography.com/people/madam-cj-walker-9522174

Madam C.J. Walker Manufacturing Company
http://en.wikipedia.org/wiki/
Madame_C.J._Walker_Manufacturing_Company

Madam Walker research at the National Archives
http://www.youtube.com/watch?v=p3qjlLYszEI

On This Day – Obituary, *The New York Times*
http://www.nytimes.com/learning/general/onthisday/bday/1223.html

Stille, Darlene R. *Madam C.J. Walker: Entrepreneur and Millionaire.*
Minneapolis, MN: Compass Books: 2007.

Women in History: Madam C.J. Walker
http://www.lkwdpl.org/wihohio/walk-mad.htm

Dorothy Shaver

Benson, Susan Porter. *Counter Cultures: Saleswomen, Managers, and Customers in American Department Stores, 1890–1940.* Chicago, IL: University of Illinois Press, 1987.

Dorothy Shaver
http://americanhistory.si.edu/archives/WIB-tour/dorothy_shaver.pdf
http://www.encyclopediaofarkansas.net/encyclopedia/
entry-detail.aspx?entryID=1762
http://www.anb.org/articles/10/10-02304.html

Fashion Group History
http://www.fgi.org/index.php?news=311

Fifth Avenue's First Lady: Dorothy Shaver
http://www.csw.ucla.edu/publications/newsletters/academic-
year-2008-09/article-pdfs/Jun09_Amerian.pdf

Sources

Harvard Business School: Leadership: Dorothy Shaver
http://www.hbs.edu/leadership/database/leaders/dorothy_shaver.html

Lord & Taylor
http://en.wikipedia.org/wiki/Lord_%26_Taylor

Sarkela, Sandra J., Susan Mallon Ross, Margaret A. Lowe, eds. *From Megaphones to Microphones: Speeches of American Women, 1920 –1960.* Westport, CT: Praeger: 2003, pp. 297– 301.

Setting the Precedent: Dorothy Shaver
http://amhistory.si.edu/archives/WIB-tour/mainMovie.html

Steamroller: Dorothy Shaver
http://www.capitalistchicks.com/?q=node/520

The art of selling style at Lord & Taylor, 1924–1945
http://www.wlv.ac.uk/default.aspx?page=23689

Webber-Hanchett, Tiffany. "Dorothy Shaver: Promoter of 'The American Look,'" in Welters, Linda and Abby Lillethun, eds. *The Fashion Reader.* Oxford, UK: Berg: 2007, pp. 369–373.

Dame Anita Roddick

Anita Roddick
http://www.anitaroddick.com/

Anita Roddick, Body Shop Founder, Dies at 64
http://www.nytimes.com/2007/09/12/world/europe/
12roddick.html?_r=0

Anita Roddick Biography
http://www.famous-women-and-beauty.com/
anita-roddick-biography.html

Anita Roddick – Mrs. Body Shop
http://www.youtube.com/watch?v=-9vylBfIpLM

The Body Shop
http://www.thebodyshop.com

Body Shop Founder & Environmental Campaigner Anita Roddick
1942-2007
http://www.democracynow.org/2007/10/22/
body_shop_founder_environmental_campaigner_anita

Great Entrepreneurs
http://www.myprimetime.com/work/ge/roddickbio/index.shtml

I Am an Activist
http://www.iamanactivist.org/

Roddick, Anita. *Business As Unusual: The Triumph of Anita Roddick*.
London, UK: Thorsons, 2000.

The Story of Anita Roddick
http://www.youtube.com/watch?v=lg7pdqPg8Uo&feature=related

Naina Lal Kidwai

Amarnath, Nischinta. *The Voyage to Excellence: The Ascent of 21
Women Leaders of India Inc.* New Delhi, India: Pustak Mahal, 2005.

Business Leaders: Naina Lal Kidwai
http://www.in.com/naina-lal-kidwai/biography-204251.html

The country head of HSBC was the first woman to enter the male bastion of investment banking
http://businesstoday.intoday.in/story/most-powerful-women-in-business-2011-naina-lal-kidwai/1/18329.html

Harvard Business School: Alumni Bulletin
http://www.alumni.hbs.edu/bulletin/2003/march/qanda.html

"I Am Gauriben ..." – Naina Lal Kidwai
http://fleximoms.in/Media/Vaahini_2/microsite.accenture.com/
vaahini/opinion/Pages/i-am-gauriben.html

India's Top Bankers
http://www.stockmarketdigital.com/ceo_profiles/indias-top-bankers

Meet the Extraordinary Naina Lal Kidwai
http://newsblaze.com/story/20110419163105iwfs.nb/topstory.html

Naina Lal Kidwai
http://en.wikipedia.org/wiki/Naina_Lal_Kidwai

Naina Lal Kidwai: Profile
http://www.terina.org/docs/naian_b.pdf

Naina Lal Kidwai's Journey
http://www.youtube.com/watch?v=fCuSJukYDK8

Naina Lal Kidwai's Mantras for Success
http://www.tribuneindia.com/2004/20040911/saturday/main1.htm

Naina Kidwai named among world's top business influentials
http://articles.timesofindia.indiatimes.com/2002-11-25/
india-business/
27293618_1_naina-lal-kidwai-hsbc-shanghai-banking-corporation

Pride of India – Naina Lal Kidwai
http://www.youtube.com/movie?v=0LTIcwVkfmA
http://www.youtube.com/watch?v=c3RCoARNv9g

Reference for Business: Naina Lal Kidwai
Naina Lal Kidwai 1957 – Biography - Breaking the glass ceiling

Spark of the Corporate: Naina Lal Kidwai
http://sparks.wisdomjobs.com/34-naina-lal-kidwai.html

Starting as the first woman employee of a big company, she is now a
top woman banker
http://www.theweekendleader.com/Success/434/prima-donna-of-
banking.html

Sheryl Sandberg

Makers: Women Who Make America: Sheryl Sandberg
http://video.pbs.org/video/2209136500/

A New Metaphor for Your Career
http://www.huffingtonpost.com/sheryl-sandberg/
class-day-speech_b_1557898.html

Facebook's Sheryl Sandberg on Women in Workplace: "Don't Leave
Before You Leave"
http://allthingsd.com/20110518/facebooks-sheryl-sandberg-on-
women-in-workplace-dont-leave-before-you-leave/

Sheryl Sandberg
http://www.crunchbase.com/person/sheryl-sandberg
http://en.wikipedia.org/wiki/Sheryl_Sandberg
http://www.in.com/sheryl-sandberg/biography-253797.html

Sheryl Sandberg: Facebook's billion-dollar brain
http://www.independent.co.uk/news/people/profiles/
sheryl-sandberg-facebooks-billiondollar-brain-7766905.html

Sheryl Sandberg Is Facebook's First Female Board Member
http://mashable.com/2012/06/25/sheryl-sandberg-board-member/

Sheryl Sandberg: Joins Facebook Board
http://online.wsj.com/article/SB10001424052702304782404577748
9003831226744.html

Sheryl Sandberg: What She Saw at The Revolution
http://www.vogue.com/magazine/article/
sheryl-sandberg-what-she-saw-at-the-revolution/#1

Sheryl Sandberg: Why We Have Too Few Women Leaders
http://www.ted.com/talks/sheryl_sandberg_why_we_have_too_few_
women_leaders.html

Video Interviews with Sheryl Sandberg, Meg Whitman & Other Female
Heroes: The Women Who Make America
http://thenextwomen.com/2012/03/12/video-interviews-sheryl-
sandberg-meg-whitman-other-female-heroes-women-who-make-
america

Why Women Want to be Entrepreneurs
http://www.inc.com/margaret-heffernan/why-women-want-to-be-
entrepreneurs.html

A Woman's Place
http://www.newyorker.com/reporting/2011/07/11/
110711fa_fact_auletta

Sue Chen

Chen, Sue. Interview with the author, Jan. 9, 2013.

Big Happiness, Small Happiness
http://blog.nawbola.org/tag/sue-chen/

Catalano, Julie, "Upwardly Mobile" (working title), *Trinity*, Winter 2012. [draft article]

Doing it for themselves – The Opportunist
http://money.cnn.com/galleries/2011/smallbusiness/1109/gallery.
most_powerful_women_entrepreneurs.fortune/8.html

Fortune's most promising women entrepreneurs
http://postcards.blogs.fortune.cnn.com/2011/09/13/
fortunes-most-promising-women-entrepreneurs/

Member Spotlight: Sue Chen and Nova Medical Products Help People
Live to the Fullest
http://www.novamedicalproducts.com/Pdfs/GoingOn/45_
NovaNAWBOJune2012.pdf

Mobility Makeover Comes to South Los Angeles, press release from
Nova Medical Products

Nova Dances to Pink – Breast Cancer Awareness
http://www.youtube.com/watch?v=9yojfSdSmeE

Nova Medical Products
www.novamedicalproducts.com

Sue Chen
http://www.zoominfo.com/#!search/profile/person?personId=21817
3947&targetid=profile

Sue Chen, Founder & CEO, Nova Medical Products: They Told Me I
Wouldn't Be Here If I Had a Brother
http://thenextwomen.com/2012/02/02/sue-chen-founder-ceo-nova-
medical-products-they-told-me-i-wouldn-t-be-here-if-i-had-broth

Sue Chen: Nova Medical Products
http://www.lohas.com/forum/speakers/sue-chen

The Walker Stalker – an Interview with Sue Chen
http://disability.about.com/od/MobilityAidsAssistiveDevices/a/
The-Walker-Stalker-An-Interview-With-Sue-Chen.htm

Susan Mashibe

African Entrepreneur Cites Help from Leading U.S. Businesswoman
http://iipdigital.usembassy.gov/st/english/
article/2012/08/20120801134001.html#axzz2AzjreJxj

Charlie's Greenroom with Susan Mashibe of Tanjet, Tanzania
http://www.charlierose.com/view/clip/12252

Emerging Global Women Entrepreneurs
http://www.forbes.com/sites/85broads/2011/09/07/
emerging-global-women-entrepreneurs/

How One Woman's Idea Revolutionised Business Aviation In East
Africa
http://www.ventures-africa.com/2012/03/desperate-for-any-job-to-
be-near-aircrafts-tanjet-was-born-in-tanzania/

The Mikocheni Report: TEDxDAR: Susan Mashibe
http://mikochenireport.blogspot.ca/2011/11/
tedxdar-susan-mashibe.html

Susan Mashibe Named Young Global Leader by World Economic
Forum
http://travelworldnews.com/2011/04/22/susan-mashibe-named-
young-global-leader-by-world-economic-forum/

Susan Mashibe
http://www.blackentrepreneurprofile.com/profile-full/archive/2011/
august/article/susan-mashibe/

Tanzania's women fuel brain gain
http://news.bbc.co.uk/2/hi/business/3995027.stm

Sources

TEDxDar: Susan Mashibe on BBC World Service
http://tedxdar.tumblr.com/post/15355286129/
susan-mashibe-imashibe-on-bbc-world-service

The women who influence our world
http://www.thecitizen.co.tz/magazines/25-woman/25395-the-
women-who-influence-our-world.html

World Economic Forum Honors TanJet Founder as 2011 Young
Global Leader
http://www.asiatraveltips.com/news11/223-SusanMashibe.shtml

Nicole Robertson

Robertson, Nicole. Interview with the author, Nov. 5 and Nov. 26,
2012.

Aboriginal Peoples Television Network: Kids
http://www.aptn.ca/pages/kids/

Aboriginal Pride
a video directed and produced by Nicole Robertson, in association
with Muskwa Productions
http://www.youtube.com/watch?v=5WfpwDkbQlg

The Alberta Chambers of Commerce – 18th Annual Alberta Business
Awards of Distinction: The Aboriginal Woman Entrepreneur Award of
Distinction
http://www.aboriginal.alberta.ca/images/woman_award.pdf

Alberta Venture: Aboriginal entrepreneurs discuss successes, challenges and the reshaping of Alberta's economic landscape
http://albertaventure.com/2010/08/
aboriginal-entrepreneurs-discuss-successes-challenges-and-the-
reshaping-of-alberta%E2%80%99s-economic-landscape/

Muskwa Productions
http://www.muskwaproductions.com

NationTalk speaks to Nicole Robertson, October 19, 2012
http://nationtalk.ca/story/nicole-robertson-a-media-specialist-and-
president-of-muskwa-productions-consulting/

Kelsey Ramsden

Ramsden, Kelsey. Interview with the author, Jan. 22, 2013.

10 inspiring success stories from top female entrepreneurs
http://www.chatelaine.com/living/budgeting/10-inspiring-success-stories-from-top-female-entrepreneurs/

Construction sector 'inhospitable' to women: Conference Board of Canada
http://www.obep.ca/pub/Construction-sector-inhospitable-to-women-Conference-Board-of-Canada.html

Different Dirt (W100 profile)
http://www.profitguide.com/manage-grow/strategy-operations/different-dirt-w100-profile-41320

Extraordinary Women TV: Kelsey Ramsden
http://www.extraordinarywomentv.com/topics/kelsey-ramsden/

Ivey Alumna Tops PROFIT/Chatelaine's W100
http://www.iveyentrepreneur.ca/index.php/programs/new_venture_project/

Kelsey Ramsden
http://kelseyramsden.ca/
http://www.canadianbusiness.com/business-news/kelsey-ramsden/

SparkPlay
http://sparkplay.com/kelsey-ramsden/

Jodi Glover

Glover, Jodi. Interview with the author, Feb. 7, 2013.

Evans, Drew on behalf of Jodi Glover. Interview with the author, Feb. 5, 2013.

2012 CWEA Finalist: Jodi Glover
http://www.womenofinfluence.ca/2012-cwea-finalist-jodi-glover/

Sources

Innovator Idol 1 Winner Read Tech Inc.
http://www.youtube.com/watch?v=IbVUWSAEYe8

Jodi Glover
http://www.youtube.com/watch?v=6V3cfA7zoUU

Jodi Glover, Real Tech Inc.'s CEO Wins 2012 RBC Canadian Women
Entrepreneur Award
http://riccentre.ca/2012/12/jodi-glover-real-tech-inc-s-ceo-wins-
2012-rbc-canadian-women-entrepreneur-award/

Ontario Ministry of Economic Development and Innovation: Water
https://www.ontariocanada.com/ontcan/1medt/econdev/en/
ed_water_successStories_TrojanUV_en.jsp

Real Tech: Clean Water, Fresh Opportunities
http://www.mri.gov.on.ca/obr/?p=713

Real Tech Inc.
www.realtech.ca

Real Tech Inc. wins Deloitte Technology Green 15™ Award the 4th
year in a row
http://realtech.ca/pr/Real%20Tech%20G15%20Press%20Release_
Nov%202012.pdf

Spotlight: Real Tech https://www.ontariocanada.com/ontcan/1medt/
smallbiz/sb_downloads/sb_yrguide_Section_C_C7_01_en.pdf

Water's Next: People
http://watercanada.net/2013/jodi-glover/

Women and Water Management: an integrated approach
http://www.unep.org/pdf/women/ChapterFive.pdf

Women of Influence: 2012 RBC Canadian Women Entrepreneur
Award Winner – Jodi Glover
http://www.youtube.com/watch?v=IdBxMq2jcnM

Acknowledgments

I gratefully acknowledge the support of the Ontario Arts Council in the creation of this work. Special thanks goes to the following institutions, companies, or individuals who generously provided gems of information and goodwill: Andrew C. Dohm, Southwestern Michigan College, Dowagiac/Niles, Michigan; Belvedere Place Development Ltd., Kelowna, British Columbia; Duncan Aviation, Kalamazoo, Michigan; Hardy Figueroa, Western Michigan University, Kalamazoo, Michigan; Jay Foster, Memorial University, St. John's, Newfoundland and Labrador; Heather Halliday, American Jewish Historical Society, New York, New York; Ian Keay, Queen's University, Kingston, Ontario; Muskwa Productions, Calgary, Alberta; Kim Marcus, HSBC, Kingston, Ontario; Nova Medical Products, Carson, California; Drew Evans, Real Tech Inc., Whitby, Ontario; Lisa Whittaker, Western Michigan University, Kalamazoo, Michigan. In addition, I am grateful for advice and suggestions from Karen Hall Barber, Adrienne Mason, Boy McLeod, Adrienne Montgomerie, Kathleen Pratt, Alec Ross, editorial intern Amanda Thomas, Steve Walton, Jessica Webb, and editor Kathryn White. I am thankful for the love, support, and enthusiasm of Carolyn Grenier, Gary Bryant, Julie Wheeler-Bryant, and Bonnie McTaggart. Finally, big hugs to my A-team of critical readers, talented chefs, weekend warriors, and understanding kindred spirits: Daryn, Zoë, and Mari Lehoux.

Photo Credits

Cover photos (L-R): Nicole Robertson photo © Nicole Robertson, Madam C.J. Walker photo courtesy A'Lelia Bundles, Jodi Glover photo © Jodi Glover, Susan Mashibe photo © Susan Mashibe

Page 5: Photo courtesy A'Lelia Bundles

Page 10: Collection of the Smithsonian National Museum of African American History & Culture, Gift from Dawn Simon Spears and Alvin Spears, Sr.

Page 13: © New York Public Library

Page 17-26: Dorothy Shaver Papers, Archives Center, National Museum of American History, Smithsonian Institution

Page 31: © Geoff Pugh / Telegraph Media Group Limited 2013

Page 40: © John Sauven

Page 43: © Eugene Skeef

Page 45: © 2013 FICCI Blog

Page 52: © Creative Commons

Page 55: © Creative Commons

Page 59: © Matthew Wittkopp

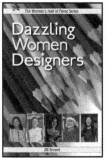

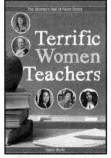

More from the Women's Hall of Fame Series

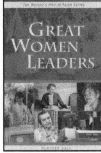

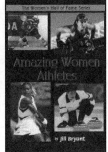

ages 9-13 • $10.95 • www.secondstorypress.ca